AFFORDABLE
ORIENTAL RUGS

ALSO BY
JANICE SUMMERS HERBERT

Oriental Rugs:
The Illustrated Guide

Affordable Oriental Rugs

THE BUYER'S GUIDE TO RUGS FROM CHINA, INDIA, PAKISTAN, AND ROMANIA

by Janice Summers Herbert

MACMILLAN PUBLISHING CO., INC.

NEW YORK

COLLIER MACMILLAN PUBLISHERS

LONDON

Macmillan Publishing Co., Inc.
866 Third Avenue, New York, N.Y. 10022
Collier Macmillan Canada, Ltd.

LIBRARY OF CONGRESS CATALOGING IN PUBLICATION DATA

Herbert, Janice Summers.
  Affordable oriental rugs.

  Bibliography: p.
  1. Rugs, Oriental.   I. Title.
NK2808.H49   746.7'5   80-43
ISBN 0-02-550170-4

Designed by Philip Grushkin

10   9   8   7   6   5   4   3   2   1

Printed in the United States of America

CONTENTS

With love

to Terry and Rusty

ACKNOWLEDGMENTS

I would like to thank the OR people throughout the world for all the help and cooperation given me in compiling this manuscript. Their dedication to the Oriental rug industry has gone far to ensure that all those interested in Oriental rugs will have accurate and up-to-date information. For their help, I am extremely grateful to:

George Bashian and Garo Bashian (Bashian Brothers Inc., New York, New York)

Jacques Bodenmann (Mori S.A., Basel, Switzerland)

Kuan-Yen Chia (Carpet Branch of China National Native Produce and Animal By-Products Import and Export Corp., Beijing, Peoples Republic of China)

Nick Ebrahimoff (Kelaty Rug Corp., New York, New York)

Kamran Etessami (Alfandari and Etessami Co., Inc., New York, New York)

Hans Felder (Oundjian S.A., Zurich, Switzerland)

Daniel Hodges (Pande, Cameron & Co., New York, New York)

Arun Kapoor and Vimal Kapoor (Kapoor Carpets, Jaipur, India)

C.M. Latif (Beco Carpets Ltd., Lahore, Pakistan)

Dimitru Oancea (ICECOOP, Carpet Dept., Bucharest, Romania)

Steven Stark (Stark Carpet Co., New York, New York)

Special thanks go to Hope Seeley for the artwork she contributed, to Richard LeNoir, Daniel Hodges, and Jack Bodenmann for their photographs, to Mia Brickley and Michele Burgess for all of their help and support. My deep appreciation also goes to the Carpet Branch of the China National Native Produce and Animal By-Products Import and Export Corporation, Romania's Carpet Department of ICECOOP, and the All India Handicrafts Board for all of the information given me.

I am especially indebted to my good friend Jacques Bodenmann of Basel, Switzerland. His vast knowledge of Oriental rugs, help, and advice have been invaluable. Jeanne Fredericks, my editor at Macmillan, has once again proved a delightful person with whom to work. For all of the help, I thank her.

My deep appreciation and love go to my son and to my husband for understanding all of the work and travel involved in putting together this book and again to my husband in particular for providing most of the line drawings. A special thank you to my mother, who chaperoned much of the travel involved in preparing this manuscript.

1

Introduction

ORIENTAL RUGS are handmade works of art in a utilitarian form. The majority of Oriental rugs today are woven in Iran, India, China, Romania, Turkey, the U.S.S.R., Afghanistan, Pakistan, and Nepal. Small numbers of Oriental rugs are also woven in Albania, Hungary, Egypt, Greece, and Morocco; these rugs do not occupy a significant portion of the Oriental rug market.

This book covers the rugs woven in India, Pakistan, China, Nepal, Tibet, and Romania. Very little published information is available on the many attributes and special qualities of these rugs. Each of these countries has a rich tradition of weaving Oriental rugs. It is my intent to provide a comprehensive review of the structural characteristics, designs, and merits of these rugs. Since they make up more than 75 percent of the Oriental rugs on the world's market, a chapter on how to purchase these affordable rugs is also included.

The economic systems in Romania, Pakistan, China, and India are such that weaving costs are relatively low. Some of the best values in Oriental rugs today are rugs woven in these countries. Many excellent-quality rugs are being woven; their designs are well executed and color combinations quite pleasing. The colors and designs of the Oriental rugs are generally available in surprisingly broad ranges to fit any decor and life-style.

THE ENDURING ART

There is a timeless beauty to the handmade art of Oriental rugs. One need not be an expert or connoisseur to appreciate and admire their harmonious colors and composition of design. Many of the designs woven into Oriental rugs may also be seen in the architecture, textiles, sculpture, tile, and frescoes of their respective areas of origin.

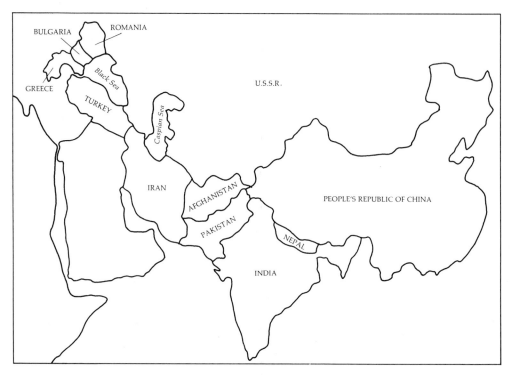

FIGURE 1-A: *ORIENTAL RUG-WEAVING COUNTRIES OF THE WORLD*

The term *Oriental rug* refers specifically to handmade rugs, which must be either hand-knotted or hand-woven. The art of carpet weaving spread across Asia, the Middle East, North Africa, and southeastern Europe through the course of numerous wars, conquests, and migrations. Each weaving center has its own history and varied means of carpet-weaving development.

No one knows exactly when or where the first hand-knotted carpets were woven. The oldest example was found in southern Siberia not far from the border of Mongolia, in the Altai Mountain valley of Pazyryk. This carpet is known as the Pazyryk carpet and is approximately twenty-five hundred years old. It has a panel design with five separate borders and its pile is knotted with the Turkish knot.

MYTH AND MYSTIQUE

The lack of information has caused many misconceptions about the Oriental rugs currently woven in India, Pakistan, China, and Romania. A wide range of designs and quality is available; these rugs may vary from excellent to inferior quality. Many times it is forgotten that the same wide range of quality is also common in the Persian (Iranian), Caucasian, and Turkish weaving centers. Consequently, one must have access to unbiased information to make the proper decision before purchasing an Oriental rug.

Another common misconception is that "no two Oriental rugs are the same." This is true in essence; however, the implication needs to be further qualified. The designs woven into the Oriental rugs of India, Pakistan, and Romania are copies of original designs of other weaving centers. Since each rug is handmade, slight variations in weave and design are inevitable. The majority of designs woven in Chinese carpets are Chinese in character, having been inspired by religious beliefs and cultural traditions. However, adaptations of French Savonnerie and Persian designs are also woven in China in Chinese carpets. No matter how skilled the weaver is, it is impossible to exactly duplicate another rug; every rug will differ.

PLATE 1.1: *PORTION OF THE WALL OF NINE DRAGONS IN THE FORBIDDEN CITY, BEIJING, CHINA*

Too often, design alone is relied on in identifying where a rug was woven. This is the result of a false presumption that each weaving center has its own unique design. The classic designs of a particular weaving center, such as the Persian town of Kashan, have long been and still are adopted and adapted by other weaving centers. The same design may be woven in many different countries and numerous weaving centers. Many of these are classic designs which have been woven for hundreds of years. While they may have once been unique to an individual weaving center, weavers from other centers often adopt these designs. For example, the Hunting design normally is associated with the Iranian town of Tabriz; but this same design is also woven in India, Pakistan, and Romania.

ORIENTAL RUGS TODAY

The Oriental carpet industry is constantly undergoing change. The availability of Oriental rugs on the world's markets are greatly affected by political instability and upheaval, industrial development, and changes in laws and tariffs. Situations internal to a country may affect the actual weaving and even the marketing of carpets once they have been completed.

Worldwide inflation has taken its toll on the Oriental carpet industry. The costs of labor and raw materials used in the weaving of rugs have soared. Even though constantly rising, labor costs are much lower in China, India, Pakistan, and Romania than in the more highly industrialized countries.

The technique of weaving has remained relatively unchanged. Weaving is still the same labor-intensive process that it has been for hundreds of years. Hundreds of thousands of individual knots are tied by hand to create a magnificent work of art.

PLATE 1.2: *DRAGON DESIGN CHINESE CARPET*

2

Construction

ALL ORIENTAL RUGS are knotted or woven by hand on a webbing formed by the warp and weft threads. *Warp* threads run vertically through the carpet, and during the weaving process are attached to the top and bottom of the loom. A strand of wool is tied around a pair of warp threads, forming a knot. The loose ends of these knots make up the body of the carpet, which is called its *pile*. *Weft* threads run horizontally ("weft" to right) through the carpet and are used to secure the knots.

PLATE 2.1: *CROSS SECTION OF AN INDIAN CARPET*

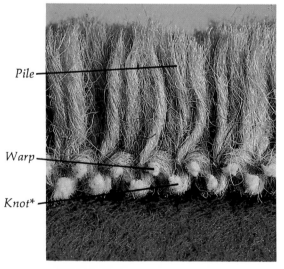

(A) *Series of Persian knots with depressed warp threads*

(B) *Illustrates the use of weft threads to secure knots*

(*yarn is looped around the depressed warp thread)

14

PLATE 2.2: *YOUNG CHILDREN WEAVING IN JAIPUR, INDIA*

WEAVING PROCESS

Portions of the weaving process vary slightly from country to country. However, the end result—a hand-knotted carpet—is still the same.

While weaving a rug, the weaver will sit for hours facing a loom upon which the warp threads are vertically strung. Depending on the size of the loom, two, three, or even four weavers may be at work at one time. Above their heads are a number of balls of varied colored yarn; each ball is made of spun wool loosely twisted together. The weaver reaches up and takes a strand of wool dangling from a ball of the desired color yarn, and this strand is then tied across a pair of warp threads. The ends of the knots are then trimmed with a small knife. The weavers are so skilled that the tying and trimming of the yarn may be done in one action. As this process is repeated across the width of the carpet, the pattern of the rug emerges.

After each row of knots has been completed, one or more weft threads are woven in and out of the warp threads. With a comblike instrument, the weft threads and knots are beaten down to secure them firmly in place. The weaver repeats this process hundreds and hundreds of times during the weaving of a carpet. The weaver will trim the ragged ends of the

PLATE 2.3: *CHINESE WEAVER
TYING A PERSIAN KNOT*

PLATE 2.4: *FINAL TRIMMING OF A CARPET IN LAHORE, PAKISTAN*

knotted yarn (pile) after several rows of knots have been tied. A final trimming is given the pile after the entire carpet has been completed.

Some Chinese and Indian carpets have pile that has been carved or sculptured. This is done after the carpet has been completed (see Plate 2.5, and Carving and Sculpturing, p. 23).

Designs are formed by the arrangements of different color strands of knotted yarn. The weaver follows a drawing called a *cartoon* or a *talim* for instructions on how to weave the rug design. Cartoons are usually drawn to scale on a piece of graphlike paper, the placement and color of each knot indicated by a single colored square. The cartoons are cut into horizontal

PLATE 2.5: *SCULPTURING OF A CARPET IN TIANJIN (TIENTSIN), CHINA*

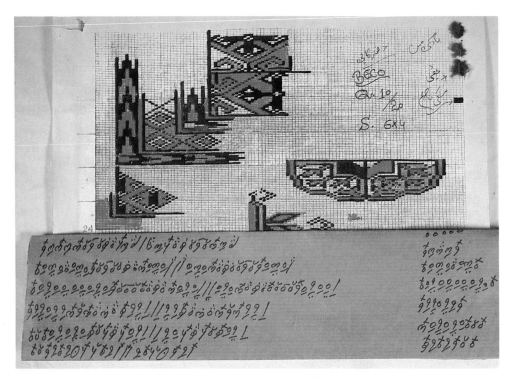

PLATE 2.6: *CARTOON AND TALIM USED IN PAKISTAN*

strips; they are mounted and varnished or enclosed in a plastic casing for protection.

In Pakistan and some parts of India, a slightly different method is used. The pattern on the cartoon is translated into a type of shorthand in a linear script form. This shorthand is a series of instructions which are read to the weavers in a singsong manner (see Plate 2.6).

The carpet ends may be finished in several different ways. The warp threads may be knotted and cut to form a fringe, by weaving a *kelim*, or by a combination of a small *kelim* with knotted fringe. The *kelim* is a strip of cloth made from weaving the weft threads back and forth through the warp threads. The fashion in which the fringes are finished is characteristic of the weaving center. For further discussion see sections on individual rugs.

The selvedges, or sides of the carpet, are secured and reinforced generally by taking the last few warp threads and wrapping them tightly with an extra overcasting of woolen yarn. Each weaving center has its own unique manner of securing the selvedge, which will be discussed under the headings for individual rugs.

LOOMS

There are two classifications of looms, the ground or horizontal loom and the upright or vertical loom. There are three types of vertical looms: the village type, the Tabriz type, and the roller beam type.

The *ground or horizontal loom* is the simplest of the looms. The warp threads are fastened to an upper and lower beam, which are held in place by stakes driven into the ground. It is used by nomadic tribes and village peasants because it is easily collapsed and may be moved from place to place. When the nomads are ready to move, the stakes are removed and the unfinished carpet is rolled around one of the beams. Once resettled, the weaver may unroll the carpet, reset the stakes, and again begin the weaving process.

The simplest of the vertical looms is the *village type*. The weaver may sit either on the ground or on a plank; the plank is raised or lowered so that the weaver is always seated directly in front of the area of the carpet on which he or she is working. The warp threads are attached to the upper and lower beams of a simple wooden frame. Although the length of the

FIGURE 2-A: *LOOMS*

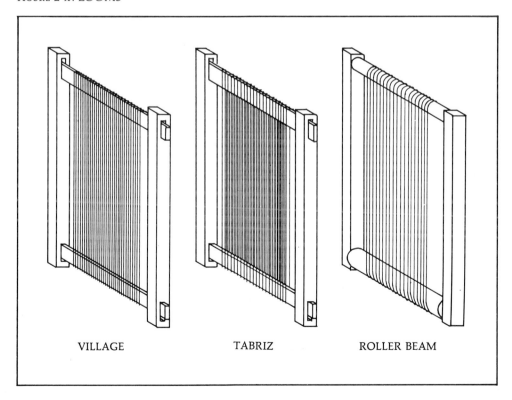

VILLAGE   TABRIZ   ROLLER BEAM

carpet is usually only as long as the distance between the upper and lower beams, it is possible to make the carpet longer by a complicated process. In this procedure the warp threads are loosened and the completed part of the rug is reattached to the lower beam. The warp threads are then retightened on the upper beam, and the weaving process is continued.

The *Tabriz type* loom, so named because it originated in the Iranian town of Tabriz, is a little more complicated than the village type. The warp threads pass in a continuous loop around the upper and lower beams. The weavers do not have to be raised with this type of loom because, as the weaving process progresses, the rug may be lowered down around the lower beam and up the back of the loom. The completed part of the carpet can then easily be inspected. With this type of loom, the length of the carpet can be made twice the distance between the upper and lower beams.

The *roller beam type* is the most advanced of the loom types. Warp threads are wound around the upper beam with their ends attached to the lower beam. As the weaving process progresses, the warp threads are unwound from the upper beam and the finished part of the carpet is rolled around the lower beam. Carpets of any length can easily be woven.

MATERIALS

The three most important materials used in the weaving of Oriental rugs are wool, cotton, and silk. The majority of Oriental rugs are woven in woolen pile; however, jute, yak and horse hair, and other animal fibers are occasionally used. The warp and weft threads of most rugs woven in China, India, and Pakistan are cotton. Silk rugs are woven in Kashmir and China; the silk pile may be woven on either a cotton or a silk foundation. In Romania, rugs are woven with either a cotton or woolen foundation in varying quality grades (see Chapter 8, Figure 8-B).

Cotton is a better fiber for the warp and weft threads than wool. It does not possess the elastic tendencies of the wool, and knots can be tied tighter to a cotton warp, yielding a more closely woven carpet. Rugs made with a cotton warp and weft are also heavier than those made with wool; as a result they lie flatter on the floor and will not "walk" or "creep."

Wools vary greatly from region to region. Many different factors affect the texture, color, quality, and durability of the wool. The breed of sheep, climate, and fall shearing or spring shearing all affect the ability of the wool to withstand wear. Some of the wool used in the rugs of India and Pakistan is imported from Australia and New Zealand. The imported wool is blended with the local and yields a stronger more lustrous carpet.

Fine textiles and carpets have been woven with silk since the earliest of times. Its great tensile strength makes silk the strongest fiber used for warp threads. The most finely knotted carpets are usually woven with silk warp threads. As a floor covering, silk pile rugs are not as durable as those woven with woolen pile. Like wool, silk has different properties depending on its area of origin. The majority of silk rugs are woven for decorative purposes.

There is a practice by which the wool of butchered sheep ("skin" or "dead" wool) is used. The animal skin is submerged in a caustic solution which allows the wool to be easily scraped from the skin. This process weakens the woolen fibers, and rugs made with this wool will show wear much faster than those made with wool shorn from living sheep. Also, skin wool does not take the dyes very well, giving the carpet a dull and lusterless appearance. With experience, skin wool can be detected; skin wool feels comparatively coarse and bristly to the touch.

KNOTS

There are two different methods of tying the spun wool, or yarn, to the warp threads. They may be tied by either a Turkish (Ghiordes) or a Persian (Senna) knot (see Figure 2-B). The tying technique of these types of knots may vary slightly from region to region, but the end result is still the same.

The nomenclature is somewhat confusing and can be misleading. For example, the Persian knot is referred to by some authors as the Senna knot, named after the ancient Iranian town of Senna. The Turkish knot is sometimes called the Ghiordes knot, so named for the small town of Ghiordes in the western Anatolian plateau of Turkey.

The *Turkish knot* is a strand of wool which encircles two warp threads, with the loose ends drawn tightly between the two warps. This is the easiest knot to tie. Rugs can be tightly woven with this knot; however, it is generally a coarser knot than the Persian knot.

The *Persian knot* is a strand of wool that encircles one warp thread and winds loosely around the other. One loose end is pulled through the two warp threads while the other emerges outside of the paired warps. The Persian knot is the more difficult of the two knots to tie and gives a more clearly defined pattern and a more tightly woven rug.

The *jufti*, or *"false,"* knot is simply a Turkish or Persian knot tied to four warp threads instead of two. The use of the *jufti* knot spread throughout the carpet-weaving industry in epidemic proportions after World War II. By using this knot, the weaver was able to tie half as many knots as would normally be required if he used the Turkish or Persian knot. Since four warp threads are used instead of two, a carpet may be woven with half the number of knots, in half the time. Pile density is halved, which yields carpet that is much less resistant to wear. The *jufti* knot is not the threat to the carpet industry that it once was.

In Tibet, the weavers use a unique method of knotting the pile. The

Cross section

Warps on same level

TURKISH
KNOT

Depressed warp

Cross section

PERSIAN KNOT

Cross section

TURKISH JUFTI KNOT

Cross section

PERSIAN JUFTI KNOT

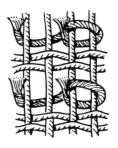

FIGURE 2-B: *KNOTS*

first and last knots of each row are tied with the Turkish knot, in the usual manner. Instead of cutting the yarn, it is looped around consecutive pairs of warp threads (similar to the Persian knot) and then around a metal or wooden rod (see Figure 2-C). This rod allows an entire row of knots to be looped without having to cut each knot individually.

After a row of knots has been completed, it is secured by several weft threads which are inserted and then beaten down. A knife is run along the rod, cutting the pile; it is then removed and another row started.

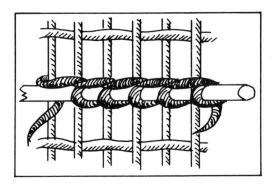

FIGURE 2-C:

TIBETAN KNOTTING TECHNIQUE

Series of Loops with initial and final Ghiordes Knots

SCULPTURING (EMBOSSING) AND CARVING

A distinguishing feature of Chinese and some Indian carpets is that of sculpturing, also referred to as embossing, and carving of the pile. Only the Chinese-design and Aubusson-design carpets of India are carved or sculptured.

A design or motif which is to be sculptured (embossed) will be woven with slightly longer pile than that of the rest of the ground. After the carpet has been completed, the raised designs will be further accentuated by trimming selective parts of the motifs. This is done on a slant to give a relief or sculptured effect to the pile (see Plate 2.5, page 17).

The carving of the design is done after the carpet has been completed. Grooves are cut into the pile outlining the borders, or surrounding the designs and motifs (see Figure 2-D).

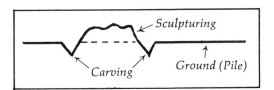

FIGURE 2-D:

CROSS SECTION OF THE PILE

DYES

The dyeing process is a delicate and complicated one. The procedure may vary slightly, depending on the substance used in making the dye. Basically, the wool is chemically treated to make it more receptive to the dye and then submerged in a vat full of boiling dye. The length of time the wool stays in the vat depends upon the type of dye and the hue desired; the wool may stay in the vat from a few hours to as long as several days. When the desired color has been attained, the wool is removed and hung in the sun to dry.

PLATE 2.7: *WOOL BEING DYED IN JAIPUR, INDIA*

Three types of dyes have been used in the dyeing of Oriental rugs: natural (vegetable or animal), aniline, and chrome. Aniline and chrome dyes are synthetic dyes.

Natural Dyes: Vegetable and Animal

Making and using natural dyes is tedious and time-consuming and can be quite expensive. The colors are derived from a number of different sources depending on what is available to the dyers. When local abundance of a natural source makes it economically feasible, vegetable or animal dyes are still used. These sources vary from country to country. The most common of the natural sources:

> *madder red—root of the madder plant; safflower*
> *cochineal red—cochineal insect*
> *yellow—weld, vine leaves, or pomegranate peel*
> *brown—walnut shells or oak bark*
> *orange—henna leaves*
> *blue—indigo plant*
> *green—combination of weld and indigo*
> *purple—hollyhocks*
> *black—gallnuts*

In older rugs there often appears a slight change of color which will run horizontally through the field of the carpet. This is called an *abrash*. This occurs when the weaver begins using yarn from a different dye lot than that previously used. With natural dyes, it is quite difficult to obtain an exact color match. This is not objectionable in itself and does not affect the value of the rug.

Aniline Dyes

The use of aniline dyes was introduced to the carpet industry in the latter half of the nineteenth century. Being easier and cheaper to use, these dyes were all too readily adopted. They were strongly acidic, which destroyed the natural oil in the wool, thus weakening the pile and causing it to wear rapidly. The colors not only faded when exposed to sunlight, but ran when washed. The use of these dyes was not limited to one area but spread throughout the rug-weaving world. Aniline dyes are not as widely used as they once were; their use is generally limited to inferior-quality rugs. In older rugs aniline dye can easily be recognized by the faded color of the pile; the back of the carpet will be much brighter than the sunlight-faded front.

To check for aniline dye in new rugs, rub a damp cloth over the pile. A good-quality vegetable or chemical dye will not rub off onto the cloth. If a color does appear on the cloth, an aniline (or other inferior) dye has been used and the rug should not be purchased.

Chrome Dyes

The majority of rugs are now dyed with what are commonly referred to as "chrome dyes." These are synthetic dyes which have been treated with potassium bichromate. In contrast to the natural dyes, chrome dyes are much cheaper to use, simpler to prepare, and their dye lots easier to match. These dyes provide a wider range of shades and colors and are colorfast; they will not fade when exposed to sunlight, or washed with water or an alkaline solution. The natural oils of the wool are not removed by the dyes, so the wearing qualities of the rug are not impaired.

The major complaint about the early chrome dyes was that their colors were harsher than the hues of the natural dyes. This problem was corrected by the use of a light chemical wash.

CHEMICAL WASH

Most rugs are given a light chemical wash before being exported. This wash simply enhances the richness of the rug and does not affect its durability.

A luster, or sheen, may be given a carpet by the chemical wash. Several factors affect the amount of luster imparted: the type of wool used for the pile and the chemical concentration of the wash. Wools vary from region to region; certain wools are more receptive to the chemical wash, gaining a more lustrous appearance than others.

An "antique" wash has been developed to give new rugs an old look. This is a rather heavy chemical wash which tones down the colors and gives the impression of being an antique rug. Rugs with an "antique" wash can be detected by splitting the pile and examining its base. The top of the pile will have a drabber, muter color than the base. The wash also gives the fringes a brownish cast.

3

Design

THE DESIGNS and their variations woven in Oriental rugs are so numerous that it is impossible to describe them all. New designs are constantly being developed; some of these are adaptations of the classic designs, while others are new patterns created by skilled designers.

The variations in design occur in the two main parts of the rug: the *field* (or *ground*), and the *borders*, which frame the interior (the field of the carpet). Designs can be divided into two different categories: curvilinear and rectilinear (see Plates 3.1 and 3.2). *Curvilinear* designs have motifs and patterns with curved outlines; *rectilinear* designs have geometric or angular motifs and patterns. These two categories may be further classified by the type of design or pattern that occupies the field: medallion, repeated motif, all-over, and prayer.

MEDALLION

The medallion rug has a field dominated by either a single central medallion or by several medallions. The field surrounding the medallion may be "open" (empty), filled, or semi-filled (small motifs scattered throughout the field). See Plate 3.3.

REPEATED MOTIF

A rug with a repeated design will have the central field filled with multiple rows of the same small motif. The Herati, Gul, and Boteh are the most common examples of this type of design (see Figure 3-A).

PLATE 3.1: *CURVILINEAR. Medallion design with open field (Romania)*

PLATE 3.2: *RECTILINEAR. Medallion design with filled field (Romania)*

PLATE 3.3:
MEDALLION DESIGN (Nepal)

Herati

The Herati pattern consists of a small rosette, generally found inside a diamond shape, surrounded by four leaves or "fish." The Herati is one of the most popular Oriental rug patterns. Romanian and Indian rugs often have excellent examples of this type of design (see Figure 3-A).

FIGURE 3-A: *REPEATED MOTIFS*

PLATE 3.4: *REPEATED MOTIF (India)*

Gul

Guls are small rectilinear emblems which were once characteristic of the Turkoman tribe that wove them. Of the Turkoman *guls*, the Tekke tribal *gul* has been the most widely used by the weaving centers of Pakistan and India (see Figure 3-A). Rugs woven in India and Pakistan with this *gul* are commonly referred to as *Bukharas** (see Plate 3.4).

Boteh

The Boteh design is one of the most widespread of the Oriental rug designs. The Boteh (paisley) design contains multiple rows of small motifs that resemble a pine cone or pear (see Figure 3-A). Many rugs with a repeated Boteh design are woven in India.

ALL-OVER DESIGN

The all-over design has a field filled with a pattern that has neither a "repeated" nor a regimented form. In contrast, the "repeated" design fills the field with multiple rows of a single motif. An all-over design has very little repetition and a large scaled pattern that fills the field. Examples of the all-over designs are Shah Abbas, Garden or Hunting, Tree or Vase, Panel, and Picture.

Shah Abbas

The Shah Abbas pattern, named for the patron of Persian carpet-making, is floral in character. The field is filled with palmettes and vases, interspersed within an intricate network of tendrils. The Shah Abbas patterns woven in the rugs from Romania, India, and Pakistan are beautifully executed copies of Persian rugs from Isfahan, Kashan, and Tabriz (see Plate 3.5).

Garden or Hunting

The Garden or Hunting pattern represents a nature scene; combinations of trees, flowers, animals, birds, and human figures fill the field. The Hunting design is a variation of the Garden pattern, with a hunter (usually with a

---

* Janice Herbert, *Oriental Rugs: The Illustrated Guide* (New York: Macmillan Pub. Co., Inc., 1978), pp. 110–22.

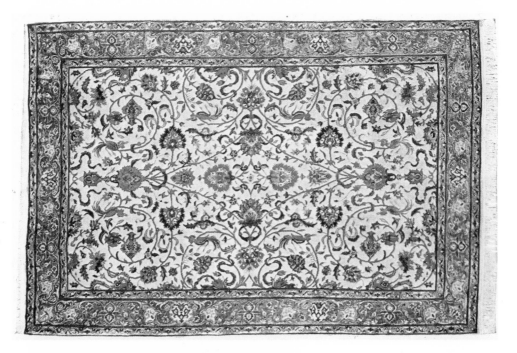

PLATE 3.5: *SHAH ABBAS DESIGN (Romania)*

PLATE 3.6: *HUNTING DESIGN (India)*

33

bow and arrow) having been added. Garden and Hunting designs are woven in rugs from India, Pakistan, and Romania (see Plate 3.6).

Tree or Vase

The Tree or Vase design has been widely adopted by many weaving centers. This design has a tree or vase from which emanate tendrils or branches. The branches generally have flowers, leaves, or pomegranate fruits which help fill the field. In the Xinjiang province of China, one of the most commonly woven designs is a Tree design with pomegranate fruits. Vase-design carpets, which are copied from the Persian rugs of Kashan, are woven in Kashmir (see Plate 3.7).

Panel

Panel-design carpets are easily recognized by the rectangular compartments ("panels") into which the field is divided. Each compartment encloses one of a variety of motifs. Romania, Pakistan, and India all weave excellent copies of the Persian designs (see Plate 3.8).

Picture

Picture carpets are those in which portraits or scenes are woven. Like a painting, picture carpets realistically portray a specific person, still life, or landscape. Tapestry-like rugs with scenic landscapes are woven in China; and in Romania a tapestry-type rug is woven with a design reminiscent of old French tapestries. Portrait carpets are woven in both India and Pakistan (see Plate 3.9).

PLATE 3.8: *PANEL DESIGN (India)*

PLATE 3.9: *PICTURE CARPET (China)*

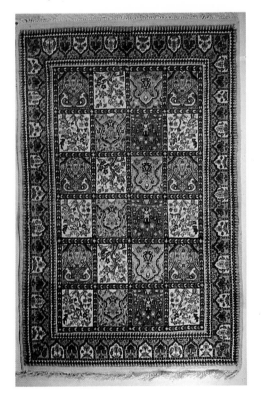

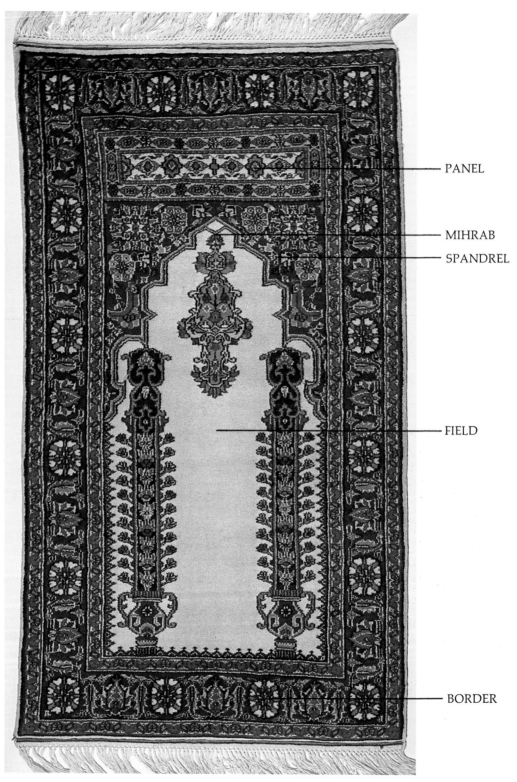

PANEL

MIHRAB

SPANDREL

FIELD

BORDER

PLATE 3.10: *DESIGN AREAS OF A PRAYER RUG (India)*

PRAYER RUGS

Prayer rugs are easily identifiable by the prayer niche (*mihrab*) or arch present (see Plate 3.10). This arch may be either geometric or curvilinear; the prayer niche is either empty, or filled with various motifs common to the area from which the pattern was adopted. Prayer rugs have been woven throughout Turkey, Iran, the Caucasus region, and both eastern and western Turkestan. Copies of these traditional patterns are woven in Pakistan, India, and Romania.

Rugs with multiple *mihrabs* are referred to as *Saffs*. They are woven in Eastern Turkestan (Xinjiang, or Sinkiang, province of China) and Turkey. Copies of the Turkish Saff are now being woven in Pakistan (see Plate 3.11).

BORDERS

A series of borders or "frames" surround and set off the interior and major attraction of the carpet, its ground or field. Just as the field designs and motifs vary, the borders also differ. Borders are not limited to particular types of rugs, designs, or origin; they are freely borrowed, adopted, and adapted for each area's own use. For example, a Herati border from a Persian Herez may be copied in a Herez-design rug from India, Pakistan, or Romania. Some of the most commonly used border designs are illustrated in Figures 3-B and 3-C.

China has its own tradition of designs and motifs. Chinese border designs are unique and may be seen in other forms of Chinese art, such as pottery, sculpture, or silk brocades. The Key and Running T border designs are often interchanged for either a major or minor border (see Figure 3-B for commonly used Chinese borders).

PLATE 3.11: *SAFF DESIGN (Pakistan)*

The number of borders vary, usually from three to seven, depending on the size, design, or origin of the rug. Some Chinese rugs are woven with no border at all, while others may have only one. The majority of Oriental rugs have a single main border (*Ara-Khachi*), flanked by matching smaller borders (*Bala-Khachi*). The major and minor borders may be further separated by lines or by even smaller borders. Aubusson-design rugs woven in India and Esthetic-design rugs woven in China have a unique floral-type border. This border arrangement has curved and scalloped outlines rather than a regimented form (see Plate 4.9).

The same border designs should appear on all four sides of the rug. Turkoman and Turkoman-design (Bukhara) rugs are the only exceptions, since they often have dissimilar side and end borders. An additional panel, called a *skirt*, is woven at the top and bottom of these rugs (see Plate 3.4).

FIGURE 3-B: *MAJOR BORDER DESIGNS*

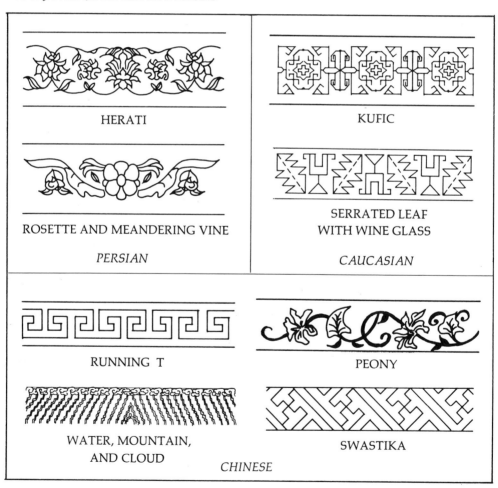

HERATI

KUFIC

ROSETTE AND MEANDERING VINE

SERRATED LEAF
WITH WINE GLASS

PERSIAN

CAUCASIAN

RUNNING T

PEONY

WATER, MOUNTAIN,
AND CLOUD

SWASTIKA

CHINESE

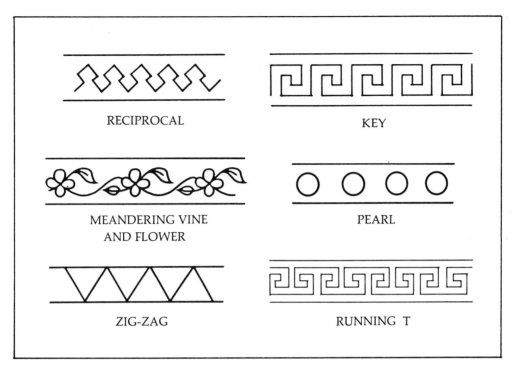

FIGURE 3-C: *MINOR BORDER DESIGNS*

SYMBOLISM

During the several thousand years of Oriental rug weaving, many different designs and motifs have been woven. Through local legends and religion, many of these designs have gained special symbolic significance. Colors may also represent special meanings. Several weaving centers sometimes attached a common meaning to individual motifs; even so, the meanings of the same motifs varied slightly.

Because of the natures of development of the Oriental rug industry in Romania, India, and Pakistan, their uses of designs and motifs have no inherent or traditional symbolic meaning. Romanian, Indian, and Pakistani designs and motifs are borrowed from other weaving centers, particularly Iran (Persia), Turkestan, the Caucasus region, and China. Traditional motifs and colors and their meanings are illustrated in Figure 3-D.

Symbolism has played an important part of the designs woven in Chinese and Tibetan rugs. Over the years, meanings became attached to certain motifs by ancient legends, traditions, and religions. For a detailed discussion of Chinese symbolism, see page 45, and for the Buddhist symbols used in Tibetan rugs see Figure 4-D, page 47.

TREE-OF-LIFE
(Eternal life)

CYPRESS TREE
(Life after death)

WEEPING WILLOW
(Sorrow, Death)

POMEGRANATE
(Fertility, Riches)

CAMEL
(Wealth, Happiness)

PEACOCK
(Sacred bird)

DOG
(Vigilance)

DOVE
(Peace)

LION
(Power, Victory)

COLOR	INTERPRETATION	COLOR	INTERPRETATION
RED	*Happiness, Joy*	BLACK	*Destruction*
BLUE	*Solitude, Truth*	ORANGE	*Devotion, Piety*
WHITE	*Purity, Peace, Grief*	YELLOW	*Power, Glory*
BROWN	*Fertility*	GREEN	*Paradise, "Prophet's Color," Sacred Color*

FIGURE 3-D: *TRADITIONAL INTERPRETATION OF MOTIFS AND COLORS*

4

The Rugs
of China

CHINA IS ONE of the world's oldest civilizations, a land steeped in tradition. Its written history covers thirty-five hundred years. The country was unified into a nation two thousand years ago. Through the course of wars and revolutions, many dynasties and governments ruled China until 1949, when the People's Republic of China was formed.

Chinese art reached high forms of development as early as the third century B.C. Sculptures and bronzes have been found which were made thirty-five hundred years ago; tempera paintings on silk and wood two thousand years old are still in existence. The emergence of hand-knotted carpets, however, appeared relatively late in Chinese history.

There are many theories on the origin of Chinese carpets. The earliest Chinese carpets were made of felt about two thousand years ago, but these carpets were not hand-knotted. The first uses of carpets were utilitarian— as floor and seat covers. Poems written during the early Han dynasty (206 B.C. to 20 B.C.) refer to the emperor and other members of the Imperial Court sitting on carpets.

The first hand-knotted carpets appeared in China with the eastward wanderings of nomads from Xianjiang (Sinkiang) and central Asia. These nomads used their carpets as seats, mats, and bedding.

Early Chinese rugs followed the utilitarian uses of the nomads, especially as bedding and *k'ang* covers. The *k'ang* was very similar in use to modern couches, although it resembled a long low table. The *k'ang* was

---

The new Pinyin spellings of Chinese place names used in this chapter are accompanied at first mention by the traditional spelling, which follows in parentheses.

raised from the floor as protection from the cold and dampness. In the homes of the poorer Chinese, *k'angs* were made of mud or bricks; fires were often built under them against the cold. Later *k'angs*, and those used in the homes of the wealthier Chinese, often were made of wood and were very elaborate. Much time was spent on the family *k'ang*, sleeping and eating. Covers made the *k'ang* more comfortable, and hand-knotted carpets found an early use in this purpose. Hand-knotted carpets were also used as seat covers, bedding, saddle blankets, covers for temple pillars, as well as floor coverings.

The greatest development in ancient Chinese carpet-weaving occurred under the patronage of the Emperor Ch'ien Lung, who reigned from 1735 to 1796. A number of seventeenth-century carpets have been found and a few specimens are believed to have been woven before 1600 A.D.

In 1871, the Ching Emperor T'ung Chih established a technical school for carpet-weaving in Beijing (Peking). Llamas were brought from the Gansu (Kansu) province to Beijing to serve as the teachers in the fine art of carpet-weaving.

It was not until the early part of the twentieth century that appreciable foreign demand for Chinese rugs began. American interest began about

FIGURE 4-A: *CHINA*

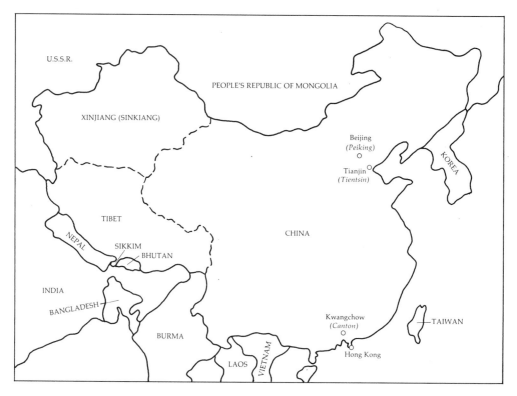

1915, and Europe soon followed after the end of World War I. Weaving establishments sprang up overnight in China to meet the surge in demand; Beijing and Tianjin (Tientsin) became the primary manufacturing centers. Many rugs were woven specifically for export; their designs were influenced by foreign tastes.

The Chinese wove rugs during this period for their own use, too, but these were quite different from those woven for export. Weavers chose designs and symbols that were relevant to or had special meaning to them. If the rug was being commissioned as a present, designs appropriate for the occasion were used. A pine tree and deer (symbols for a good, safe journey) would be woven in a carpet to be given as a going-away present.

The Chinese carpet as we know it today first appeared in the mid-1920s. In many ways it is similar in construction to that of its predecessors. The Persian knot is used on a foundation which is either cotton or silk. Wool pile rugs always have a cotton foundation; silk pile rugs may have either an all-silk foundation or a foundation made of cotton warps and silk wefts.

The modern Chinese rugs have standardized quality ranges; countless numbers of stock designs, color combinations, and sizes are available.

The Chinese are masters at the art of using colors, even though the total number of colors in a rug might be very limited. Their use of graduated shades of the same color is unique among weaving centers; as many as ten different shades of the same color may be found in a single rug.

SYMBOLISM

For more than a thousand years, symbolism has played an important part in all forms of Chinese art, including that of rug weaving. To fully appreciate Chinese rugs, it is very helpful to understand some of the symbolism behind their designs and motifs. Chinese rugs contain designs with symbolic representations from nature, ancient legends and traditions, and the Buddhist and Taoist religions (see Figure 4-B).

FIGURE 4-B: *CHINESE MOTIFS AND THEIR INTERPRETATIONS*

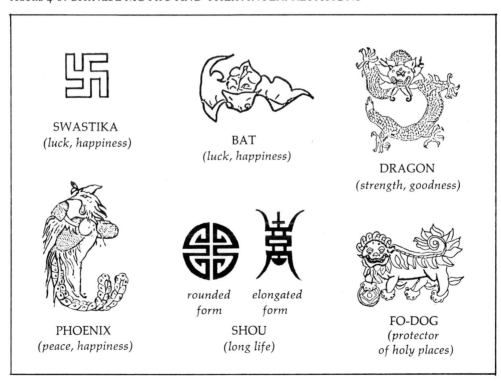

SWASTIKA
(*luck, happiness*)

BAT
(*luck, happiness*)

DRAGON
(*strength, goodness*)

PHOENIX
(*peace, happiness*)

rounded
form

elongated
form

SHOU
(*long life*)

FO-DOG
(*protector
of holy places*)

FAN
*(Reviving souls of
the departed)*

SWORD
(Supernatural power)

BASKET OF FLOWERS
*(Supernatural power
through blossoms)*

BAMBOO
(Telling fortunes)

STAFF AND GOURD
(Transmutation)

CASTANETS
(Soothing influence)

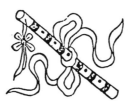

FLUTE
(Performing magic)

LOTUS POD
(All-powerful)

FIGURE 4-C: *SYMBOLS OF TAOISM*

WHEEL
(Majesty of the law)

CONCH SHELL
(Calling to prayer)

UMBRELLA
(Esteem, Dignity)

CANOPY
(Protection)

LOTUS FLOWER
(Purity)

VASE
(Enduring peace)

FISHES
(Abundance)

KNOT
(Knot of destiny)

FIGURE 4-D: *SYMBOLS OF BUDDHISM*

In the Taoist religion there was a belief in Eight Immortals; they were virtuous people who were rewarded with immortality. Each spirit was believed to possess supernatural powers. Occasionally these immortals were given human form and were pictured with the symbols of their attributes (see Plate 4.5). More often, they were not pictured in their human form but were represented only by the symbols of the attributes (see Figure 4-C).

The Buddhist religion had eight other symbols with significant meaning, each symbol being a happy prophecy or omen of Buddhist belief (see Figure 4-D). The Fo-dog is also of Buddhist origin. The *fo*, which resembles more a lion than a dog, was believed to be the defender of the law and protector of the temples and holy places. Fo-dogs are sometimes seen in pairs; the male is depicted with a ball and the female is pictured with a puppy (see Plate 4.6).

In some instances, meanings become attached to certain motifs because of the language or phonetics. The Chinese language has many rebuses, words that are spelled differently (different characters) but are pronounced in the same way. For example, the Chinese word for *bat* is *fu* and the word for *happiness* is also *fu* (each a different character in Chinese script), pronounced the same; consequently, the bat became used to represent happiness. This representation of a word or phrase by motifs is quite common in the Chinese language.

The number, color, shape, combination, and setting of the various representations also affected the symbolic interpretation. A stag (symbol for well-being and financial reward) was often pictured with a stork (symbol for long life); woven together they represented a prosperous long life. The single bat symbolizes happiness; the *shou*-sign represents long life. A group of four or five bats surrounding a central *shou* medallion signifies the five great blessings: long life, riches, health, virtue, and happy death (see Plate 4.2).

One of the best-known designs is that of the dragon, a symbol of the Imperial ruler. There were several types of dragons; the Imperial dragon was depicted with five claws, the four-claw dragon was used for less important royalty, and the three-claw dragon was for the common people.

Border design also had symbolic meaning. The single swastika symbolizes happiness or luck; when attached in a series, as in a border, for example, the swastika means ten-thousand-fold happiness.

DESIGNS

Chinese rugs do not have designs that are unique or characteristic of the village, tribe, or religion where they are woven. Like other forms of Chinese art, the designs are inspired by religious beliefs and cultural traditions.

The designs of Chinese rugs are not nearly so elaborate and ornate as

PLATE 4.3:
CHINESE CARPET,
from Suiyan,
Nei Monggol
(Inner Mongolia)
Late nineteenth century
2 ft. by 4 ft.
Courtesy of
Mrs. Russell Summers

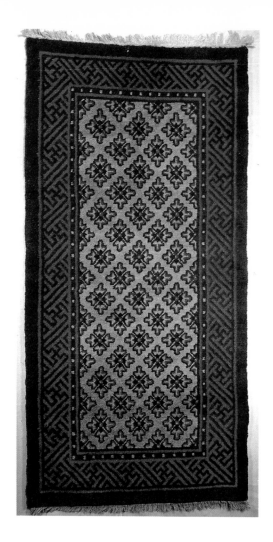

PLATE 4.4: *CHINESE CARPET, from Suiyan,*
Nei Monggol (Inner Mongolia)
Late nineteenth century
2 ft. by 4 ft.
Courtesy of Dr. Theodore T. Herbert

PLATE 4.5: *TAOIST IMMORTALS*
2 ft. by 5 ft.
Courtesy of Dr. and Mrs. Robert Marsico

PLATE 4.6: *FO-DOG*
1 ft. 6 in. by 1 ft. 6 in.
Courtesy of Mr. and
Mrs. Paul Roberts

those from other weaving centers. Their designs are crisp and well defined; the patterns are well proportioned.

The Chinese classify their rugs by the nature of the designs used. The four major classifications are Esthetic, Peking,* Floral, and Self-Tone Embossed.

Esthetic Design

The Esthetic design was developed in the 1920s for the export market. These rugs are ornate and very formal in appearance; they were adopted from the designs of the French Aubusson rugs. The central medallion generally contains a large floral spray and the borders are often scalloped (see Plate 4.7). The use of sculpturing further accentuates the designs and motifs.

Peking Design

The designs and motifs used in Peking-design rugs are inspired by ancient traditions, religious beliefs, and other symbols of the Chinese heritage. They were copied from ancient forms of Chinese art, such as sculpture, textiles, tile work, bronzes, and lacquerware (see Plates 4.8 and 4.9). Peking designs may be further classified by the type of motif used. They are Antique Design, Antique Finished, Brocade, Bronze, Bird and Flower, Figure, and Tendril.

---

* Peking, the traditional word for the city *Beijing,* will be retained when used as a design term rather than as a place name.

opposite,
PLATE 4.7: *ESTHETIC DESIGN*
3 ft. by 5 ft.
Courtesy of Miss Polly Price

PLATE 4.8: *PEKING DESIGN*
2 ft. 3 in. by 4 ft. 6 in.
Courtesy of Mr. and
Mrs. R.H. Bockbrader

ANTIQUE DESIGN

The designs and motifs in Antique Design carpets are based on figures found in different forms of Chinese art dating as early as the fourteenth century B.C. The patterns are taken from bronzes, ceramics, porcelain, lacquerware, textiles, sculpture, bricks and tiles, and antique carpets.

ANTIQUE FINISHED

Antique Finished carpets are different from those labeled as Antique Design. The designs and color combinations used in Antique Finished car-

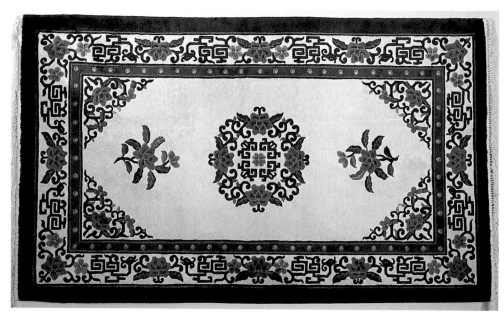

PLATE 4.9: *PEKING DESIGN, All-silk, 3 ft. by 5 ft.,*
Courtesy of Mrs. Russell Summers

PLATE 4.10: *ANTIQUE FINISHED*

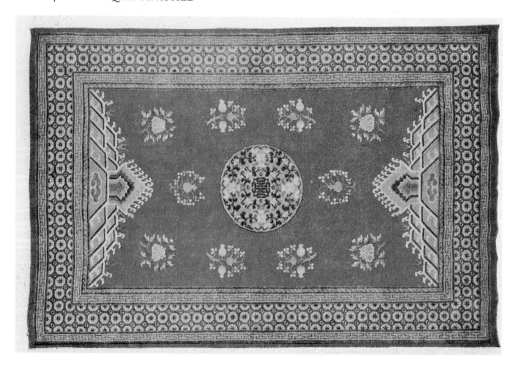

pets are duplicates of those of the Ming and Ching dynasties. These carpets are given an antique wash to give them an aged appearance (see Plate 4.10).

BROCADE DESIGN

The Brocade is a relatively new type of design, having been introduced in 1974. These designs are heavily embellished with flower and leaf motifs copied from those found in Chinese flower-figured satins (see Plate 4.11).

BRONZE DESIGN

The Bronze design bases its motifs and patterns on those found on bronzeware made from the fourteenth century B.C. to the third century B.C. These patterns were influenced by legends and mythological beasts, such as dragons and the phoenix.

BIRD AND FLOWER DESIGN

The Bird and Flower designs are based on the realistic paintings developed to a high art between the tenth and thirteenth centuries A.D. (see Plate 4.12).

PLATE 4.11:
BROCADE DESIGN

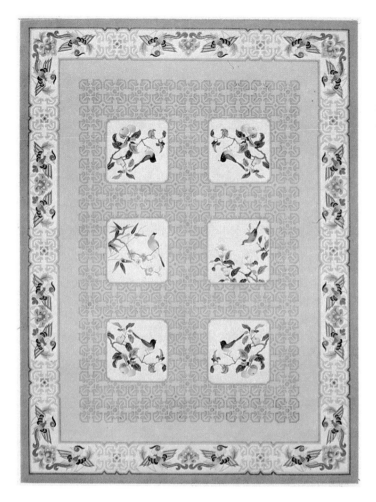

FIGURE DESIGN

The main motifs found in the Figure Design carpets are based on tracings or rubbings of figures carved on stone and brick between the third century B.C. and the third century A.D. These figures are used as a central medallion or occupy a predominant position in the field of the rug (see Plate 4.13).

TENDRIL DESIGN

The Tendril-type design is based on patterns developed between the sixth and tenth centuries A.D. Complex swirls of tendrils dominate the field, surrounding a central medallion (see Plate 4.14).

PLATE 4.13:
FIGURE DESIGN

PLATE 4.14:
TENDRIL DESIGN

Floral

The Floral design was developed in the 1920s for the American market. This type of design has no borders. Floral sprays and individual blossoms are scattered across the rug in such a fashion that they appear to be placed randomly (see Plates 4.15 and 4.16).

Self-Tone Embossed

The Self-Tone Embossed design is also called the Plain design. These rugs are monochromatic. The designs and motifs are carved or embossed onto the rug, being accentuated by the relief effect. The designs of the Esthetic and Floral rugs are used commonly in the Self-Tone Embossed rugs.

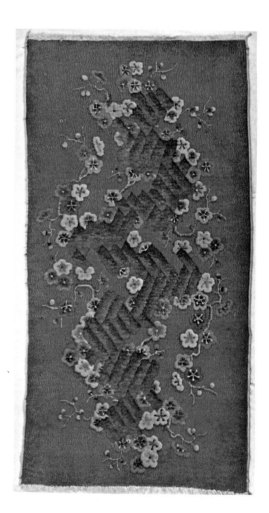

PLATE 4.15: *FLORAL DESIGN*
2 ft. 11 in. by 5 ft. 8 in.
Courtesy of Mr. and Mrs. Donald Dieterich

PLATE 4.16: *FLORAL DESIGN*
3 ft. diameter
Courtesy of Mrs. Harry Mitman

PLATE 4.17: *MINZU DESIGN*

Minzu

The Minzu design was developed in 1976 to recognize the diversity of the Chinese cultural heritage. The motifs and patterns are inspired by those drawn from the many minorities comprising the Chinese people (see Plate 4.17).

STRUCTURAL CHARACTERISTICS

The standard practice is to describe a Chinese rug according to each item in a group of structural variables:

line quality
machine-spun or hand-spun wool
length of pile
open or closed back
pile treatment

The most popular type of Chinese rug on both the European and American markets is known as the "Super Chinese." Its structural characteristics are ⅝-inch pile, 90-line, machine-spun wool, closed back, and hand-carved pile. The structural combinations normally available in Chinese rugs are identified in Figure 4-E.

Rug quality is identified by *line*, a terminology somewhat different from that used in most weaving centers. *Line* equals the number of pairs of warp threads, or knots per linear foot. A 90-line rug has 90 knots per linear foot, which is approximately equivalent to 56 knots per square inch. The line quality available in wool rugs is 70, 90, 120, 240, and occasionally even higher.

PILE CHARACTERISTICS			OPEN BACK		CLOSED BACK		
PILE HEIGHT	NUMBER OF PLIES IN WOOL PILE YARN		70 LINE	90 LINE	90 LINE	120 LINE	240 LINE
⅜"	4						x
⅜"	4		x	x		x	x
⅜"	4		x	x		x	
⅝"	5			x	x		

FIGURE 4-E: *STRUCTURAL COMBINATIONS OF CHINESE RUGS*

LINE QUALITY	KNOTS PER SQUARE INCH	APPROX. KNOTS PER SQUARE METER
70	34	52,750
90	56	87,000
120	100	155,000
240	400	620,000

TABLE 4-E-1: *LINE QUALITY CONVERSION CHART*

PLATE 4.18:
CLOSED BACK WEAVE
90-Line Quality

PLATE 4.19:
OPEN BACK WEAVE
90-Line Quality

Chinese wool is more delicate than that used in the rugs of Iran. However, this is compensated for in the construction of the Chinese rugs by increasing the number of ply in the yarn used for the tying of the knots, and by the thickness and length of the pile.

The wool used for the pile is spun either by machine or by hand. The majority of rugs have machine-spun wool. Machine-spun wool is more even, uniform, resilient, and yields a more durable carpet. A 90-line carpet has approximately 550 grams (1.2 pounds) of machine-spun wool per square foot.

The normal length of the pile is either $\frac{3}{8}$, $\frac{4}{8}$, or $\frac{5}{8}$ inch; while $\frac{4}{8}$ does equal $\frac{1}{2}$ inch, for consistency all lengths are quoted in eighths. Very finely knotted rugs (240-line or more) occasionally have a pile thickness of only $\frac{2}{8}$ inch. Silk rugs generally have $\frac{2}{8}$-inch pile.

The appearance of the back of the rug is the basis of another group of structural variables: open back or closed back. *Open back* rugs have weft threads that are clearly visible from the back of the rug. On *closed back* rugs the weft threads are not visible from the back; the knots completely cover the weft threads (see Plates 4.18 and 4.19). Because of the depression of the warp threads and the manner in which the knots are tied, more wool is required on closed back rugs. Approximately 20 percent more wool is used in a 90-line closed back rug than in the same size 90-line rug with an open back.

Another distinguishing feature of Chinese carpet structure is that of embossing and carving of the pile. An embossed or sculptured design will be woven with slightly longer pile than that of the rest of the ground. After the carpet has been completed, the raised designs will be further accentuated by trimming selective parts of the motif. This is done on a slant to give a relief or sculptured effect to the pile (see Plate 4.20).

This same technique is used on a unicolor rug; the motif or design will be woven with the same color as the ground. The pile of the designs may be woven either higher or lower than that of the rest of the ground. Further trimming is done when the carpet has been removed from the loom.

The carving of the design is done once the rug has been completed. Grooves are cut into the pile outlining borders, or surrounding designs.

PLATE 4.20:
SCULPTURED PILE

WEAVING CENTERS

The weaving industry of China is now directed by the Carpet Branch of the China National Native Produce and Animal By-Products Import and Export Corporation. There are seven major carpet-weaving branches which are located in Beijing, Shanghai, Hebei (Hopeh), Shandong (Shantung), Dalein (Tailien), Tianjin (Tientsin), and Xinjiang (Sinkiang). Each branch has its own specialized area of rug production, with numerous factories within each branch. Beijing, Shanghai, and Tianjin are also major centers for the export of Chinese carpets.

Beijing *(Peking)*

Beijing is the oldest and one of the largest carpet-weaving branches. Many of China's best weavers were brought hundreds of years ago to Beijing to weave fine-quality carpets for the Imperial courts.

The carpets produced by the Beijing branch vary widely. Much of the production is in the 90- and 70-line qualities, with an open back, and ⅜- and ⅘-inch pile. The 90-line "Super Chinese" and a finer (120-line) quality are also woven. The carpets woven in Beijing are marketed under the "Temple of Heaven" brand name.

The standard classifications of Chinese designs are woven by the Beijing branch. In addition, some designs are made which are unique to the Beijing branch, such as the Antique, Antique Finished, Brocade, and Minzu designs. Each of these is discussed in the design section in this chapter.

Shanghai *(Shanghai)*

Shanghai is a major center for both the weaving and export of Chinese carpets. Rugs woven in Shanghai are labeled with the "Pine and Crane" brand name. Shanghai specializes in the production of wool rugs in 90- and 70-line qualities. The 90-line quality may be woven with a combination of either hand-spun or machine-spun wool, and open or closed back. The 70-line quality will be woven with an open back and hand-spun wool. The pile heights of ⅜, ⅘, and ⅝ inch are woven in both qualities. The four basic design classifications are found in the wool carpets of Shanghai.

Silk rugs are woven in Shanghai and they too are sold with the "Pine and Crane" brand name. The designs woven in the silk rugs are basically Peking designs, copies of ancient embroideries, Chinese characters, tiles and mosaics, and other historical designs.

Hebei *(Hopeh)*

Production of the Hebei branch is very similar to that of Shanghai. The carpets of this branch are sold with the "Peacock" brand name. Hebei rugs are woven either with ⅜- or ⅝-inch pile and the 70- or 90-line quality. The 70-line quality has hand-spun wool and an open back; the 90-line quality rugs have machine-spun wool, ⅝-inch pile, and either an open or closed back.

Shandong *(Shantung)*

Shandong specializes in weaving a finely knotted rug that employs a Persian-type design. These designs resemble those of Isfahan and Nain; they have central medallions and a field filled with vines and small floral motifs. Shandong rugs are finely woven in the 120- or 240-line qualities with ²⁄₈- or ⅜-inch pile. The short pile is necessary to give crisp, intricate designs.

The Shandong branch markets its rugs under the "Sea Gull" brand name. The marketing center of the Shandong branch is Tsing-tao.

Dalein *(Tailen)*

Rugs of the Dalein branch are known by the label "Great Wall" brand. This branch specializes in weaving rugs with undyed wool. These rugs usually have a natural-colored (ivory) ground, with designs and motifs of a natural brown or gray wool.

This branch also specializes in weaving rugs with the hair of animals other than sheep, such as goat, horse, mule, and yak. The majority of these carpets are also woven with undyed wool and are not chemically washed.

Tianjin *(Tientsin)*

The Tianjin branch is the largest and one of the oldest of the carpet branches. It emerged as a major carpet-weaving and exporting center in the last quarter of the nineteenth century. Tianjin carpets are marketed under the "Junco" label. The "Super Chinese" (90 line, ⅝-inch pile, closed back) accounts for the major portion of the Tianjin carpet production. Peking, Floral, Esthetic, and Self-Tone Embossed designs are woven, as well as several types of the Peking design that are unique to Tianjin. These are the Bronze, Figure, Tendril, Bird and Flower, and Antique carpet types.

Each of these classifications is discussed in the design section of this chapter.

Tapestry-type rugs and silk rugs are also woven in Tianjin. The tapestry rugs are finely woven with a closed back in either the 120- or 240-line quality. The silk rugs are also finely woven with the 120- or 240-line quality.

Xinjiang *(Sinkiang)*

KNOT:	*Persian*
WARP:	*cotton*
WEFT:	*cotton, wool (in older rugs); two or more*
PILE:	*silk, silky wool*
FRINGE:	*small* kelim *at both ends with looped fringe at one end and plain fringe at the other*
SELVEDGE:	*overcast with wool*

The Xinjiang province lies in the heart of central Asia, an area we refer to as Turkestan. Turkestan is a vast region which receives its name from the people of Turkish stock called Turkomans, who have inhabited the area since 500 A.D. Turkestan is divided into two parts by the Tien Shan Mountains: Turkestan proper to the west and eastern or Chinese Turkestan to the east. The majority of eastern Turkestan is located in what is now the Xinjiang province, an autonomous region within the People's Republic of China (see Figure 4-F).

FIGURE 4-F:
XINJIANG (SINKIANG)
(EASTERN TURKESTAN)

PLATE 4.21:
ANTIQUE
KHOTAN
6 ft. by 9 ft.
Courtesy of
Dr. Theodore
T. Herbert

Even though caravan routes have crossed eastern Turkestan for centuries, it has remained isolated. Parts of its great deserts are still untrodden by man. Foreign influences were few until the last half of the nineteenth century, when this region came under Chinese rule. Xinjiang's only railway was completed to Urumchi in 1965.

Older rugs from eastern Turkestan were often referred to in the West as "Samarkands"; the Chinese called them "Kansus." Located on ancient caravan routes, Samarkand was for centuries the major marketplace for rugs from this area which were destined for Europe and America. Gansu (Kansu) was the entry point for the rugs of eastern Turkestan entering China. Samarkand and Gansu, like Bukhara, were merely marketplaces; no rugs were actually woven there. Most of the weaving was done in and surrounding the towns of Khotan, Kashgar, and Yarkand. Rugs currently woven in the Xinjiang province are marketed in Beijing. They are commonly called "Sinkiangs" in Europe and "Khotans" in the United States.

Rugs of the Xinjiang province and eastern Turkestan reflect a unique combination of Chinese, Turkoman, and Caucasian influences. This blending of designs and motifs gives these rugs a strikingly different appearance.

In some of the older rugs, the colors were at times harsh. Red was the dominant color used in the ground, with a golden-yellow tone and several shades of blue used for the motifs. Other carpets had more muted tones, such as peach, light blue, gray, steel blue, brown, and gold colors. The newer carpets of Xinjiang have a pleasing combination of different shades of blue, brown, cream, and shades of rose red.

The weave in these carpets was rather coarse and the wool used was soft and not very durable. Consequently, many of the older carpets did not withstand wear very well. New carpets are much more finely woven in either a 90-line or 110-line quality. They have a much thicker and heavier pile and the open back weave. The knots are usually two-ply, yielding a much sturdier carpet than its earlier counterpart. The warp and weft threads of all new rugs are of cotton; wool was used for the weft threads in many of the older carpets.

The majority of carpets woven are in smaller sizes: 3 by 5 feet to 4 by 6 feet; a few runners and 6 by 9 feet carpets are also woven.

Designs commonly woven include the Medallion, Tree or Vase, Repeated Gul, and the Prayer. The rugs of Khotan quite often contain a medallion design resembling a flattened disc; this medallion also contains several smaller motifs. This medallion, called Ay Gul* (moon motif) in Khotan, may appear in single, double, or even triple forms (see Plate 4.21).

A pattern reminiscent of the Persian Tree-of-life design is also commonly woven in the rugs of Yarkand, Khotan, and Kashgar. This design is actually a pomegranate tree with fruit. The tree is situated usually in a vase at the base of the carpet's field (see Plate 4.22).

The Repeated Gul design is similar in pattern to the carpets of western Turkestan (Turkoman rugs). A small motif is repeated in multiple rows throughout the field of the carpet (see Plate 4.23).

The prayer rugs of this area were usually *Saffs*, rugs woven with multiple prayer *mihrabs* (niches). The fields of these *mihrabs* were either empty or, more often, filled with the Pomegranate Tree design.

The majority of rugs woven in the Xinjiang province have been and still are exported to European markets. They have been imported for years by the United States, but in relatively small numbers.

---

* Hans Bidder, *Carpets from Eastern Turkestan* (Zwemmer, 1964).

5

The Rugs of Tibet and Nepal

XIZANG *(Tibet)*

KNOT:	*Tibetan looped technique*
WARP:	*cotton (wool used in antique rugs)*
WEFT:	*cotton (wool used in rugs woven before 1950)*
PILE:	*thick, heavy wool; ridged in appearance*
FRINGE:	kelim *with looped fringe at one end*
	and kelim *with plain fringe at the other*
SELVEDGE:	*plain*

For three hundred and fifty years, Tibet was a religious kingdom, ruled by a Dalai Lama (Buddhist monk). Western influences in Tibet have been few, even though caravan routes had crossed Tibet for centuries. In 1965, Tibet became an autonomous region within the People's Republic of China. A long history of Chinese influences have been reflected in Tibetan dress and architecture, as well as their carpet designs.

Chinese-style medallion, dragon, and phoenix motifs were commonly woven in Tibetan carpets. These carpets were usually small and used not only as floor coverings, but also as saddle blankets, earth mats, seat covers, and bedding.

Antique Tibetan carpets are coarsely woven on a woolen foundation. Wool was solely used for the warp and weft threads until after World War I, when the use of cotton for the weft threads first appeared. In the early 1950s, cotton began to replace wool for the weft threads.* The newer

---

* Philip Denwood, *The Tibetan Carpet* (Warminster, England: Aris and Phillips Ltd., 1974), p. 16.

Tibetan rugs are much more finely woven than their older counterparts. The range of colors used in both new and old rugs is rather limited: red, blue, camel, brown, and yellow are the most common.

One of the most characteristic features of carpets woven in Tibet is the ridged appearance of their pile (see Plate 5.1). This is a result of the unique Tibetan method of weaving with the use of a metal or wooden rod. Instead of cutting the yarn after each knot, the yarn is looped around consecutive pairs of warp threads and then around the rod. A knife is run along the rod, cutting the pile after the entire row of knots has been completed. See Chapter 2, p. 23 for a further discussion.

Older Tibetan rugs were woven with a knot count typically lower than newer ones. A lower knot count is associated with less pile density, and hence less resistance to wear.

Antique and semiantique Tibetan carpets are rare. Today weaving in Tibet is still being done by individuals in their homes and also in state-owned factories in Lhasa (see Plate 5.2). "Tibetan" carpets are also woven by Tibetans now living in India and Nepal. Rugs woven in Tibet are marketed in Beijing and are commonly referred to as "Lhasas"; those woven in Nepal and India are marketed in both Kathmandu and Delhi and are referred to as "Tibetan."

The total output of new carpets from Tibet is small when compared with that of China. The majority of carpets from Tibet go to the wholesale market in London. Small quantities of Lhasas are available on the American market.

FIGURE 5-A: *TIBET AND NEPAL*

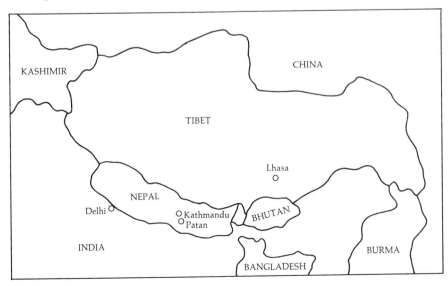

PLATE 5.1: *DETAIL OF TIBETAN PILE,*
ILLUSTRATING THE RIDGED APPEARANCE

NEPAL

KNOT:	*Persian*
WARP:	*cotton, occasionally wool*
WEFT:	*cotton, occasionally wool*
PILE:	*thick, excellent-quality wool, half-inch long*
FRINGE:	*small* kelim *at both ends with looped fringe at one end and plain fringe at the other*
SELVEDGE:	*overcast with wool*

Nepal is best known as the small kingdom at "the top of the world." It has been renowned more as the home of Mt. Everest than for the beautiful carpets woven there. Most of the rugs exported from Nepal are woven by Tibetans. Some eighty thousand Tibetans left their homeland in 1959 and 1960 for centers set up for them in India and Nepal.

Many of these refugees were experienced weavers, and by the mid-1960s carpet workshops had been set up in many of the refugee centers. These carpets are usually woven by women, are typically Tibetan in character, and are marketed as "Tibetan Carpets."

These carpets are of excellent quality and woven with Himalayan wool. Their colors are bright and designs are crisp. Designs are standardized;

PLATE 5.3:
"TIBETAN"
3 ft. by 6 ft.
Courtesy of
Miss Polly Price

Shou or floral medallions (see Plate 5.3) are commonly used, as well as the snow lion (see Plate 5.4) and other mythical symbols of their Buddhist (see Figure 4-D, p. 47) and Tibetan heritage. Even though some rugs are borderless, most will have borders; the running T or the swastika are the most common. The colors are limited in number: only twenty different colors are currently being used.

The sizes woven in "Tibetan" rugs are also standardized, 3 by 6 foot size being the most common. However, 16-inch squares for seat covers, and 4 by 7 foot, and 9 by 12 foot rugs and saddle carpets are also woven.

PLATE 5.4:
"TIBETAN"
3 ft. by 6 ft.
Courtesy of
Mrs. Richard Drbal

6

The Rugs of India

KNOT:	*Persian*
WARP:	*cotton*
WEFT:	*cotton*
PILE:	*thick, at times coarse, wool; occasionally sculptured*
FRINGE:	*loosely woven* kelim *with knotted fringe at both ends*
SELVEDGE:	*overcast with wool*

HAND-KNOTTED CARPETS have been woven in India since the sixteenth century, when the Moghul emperor, Akbar the Great, founded the Indian carpet-weaving industry. He brought Persian weavers from Kashan, Isfahan, and Kerman to his courts, and established workshops for the weaving of carpets. These carpets were very similar to those of Persia in both design and weave.

Indian carpet-weaving has had a long history of growth and recession. In 1600 the first carpet-weaving firm was founded by English merchants in Lahore, then part of India. This firm was known as the East India Carpet Company, and it soon set up other weaving workshops in Amritsar, Agra, and Delhi. The Moghul empire began to break apart soon after the death of Auranqzeb in 1707. The royal patronage of the carpet industry was brought to an end and a decline in quality quickly ensued.

A resurgence of international interest in Indian carpets was triggered by their display at the Great London Exhibition in 1851. Foreign firms again went to India, and established carpet-weaving factories in Amritsar, Srinagar, and Mirzapur. By the early part of the twentieth century, the demand for Indian carpets was so large that a carpet-weaving workshop was set up in the jail in Agra. These "convict" carpets soon became known for their fine weave. Recessions and depressions abroad before World War II caused a decline in the foreign-market demand, and the Indian rug-weaving industry was again beset by hard times.

After India gained its independence in 1947, the new government took an active interest in the carpet-weaving industry. The quality of carpet-weaving greatly improved as Indian carpet firms began to take advice and guidance from foreign Oriental carpet firms. The All India Handicrafts Board was formed in 1952 to help set high industry standards and develop the enormous potential that was as yet untapped. Schools where students can learn the art of carpet-weaving have been established in Kashmir, Rajasthan, and in Uttar Pradesh.

The majority of Indian carpets are custom-made with specified designs, colors, sizes, and quality ranges. The ability to quickly adapt designs to meet market demands as well as varying the tightness and type of weave

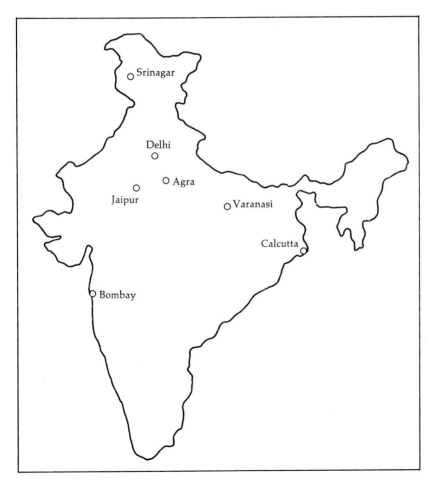

FIGURE 6-A:
INDIA

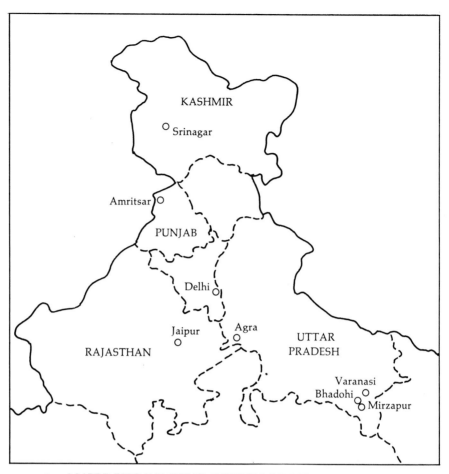

FIGURE 6-B: *MAJOR RUG-WEAVING CENTERS OF INDIA*

have given Indian rugs and carpets a competitive edge of the world's markets. Copies of Persian, Turkish, Caucasian, Turkoman, French Savonnerie, and Chinese carpets are all woven in India. During the United States trade embargo of China in the 1950s and 1960s, Indian carpet-makers responded quickly, weaving thousands of Chinese-design carpets. A shift to Persian designs began in the early 1970s as Persian carpet prices rapidly rose.

Currently, the major weaving centers in India are the Mirzapur-Bhadohi area and Agra in Uttar Pradesh, Jaipur in Rajasthan, Srinagar in Kashmir, and Amritsar in Punjab. The Mirzapur-Bhadohi area alone accounts for almost 90 percent of India's total carpet production. Rugs are woven in other areas scattered throughout India, but their total output is relatively small.

Ninety percent of all the hand-knotted carpets made in India are woven in the state of Uttar Pradesh, with the weaving scattered over five hundred towns and villages. The highest concentration of weaving is done in the eastern districts; this area is known to the carpet world as the "Mirzapur-Bhadohi Belt," and includes the towns of Varanasi, Mirzapur, Bhadohi, and Allahabad.

The weaving of carpets began in the Mirzapur-Bhadohi area approximately four hundred years ago. According to local legend, a Persian weaver was traveling with a caravan along the Grand Trunk Road. The caravan was set upon by robbers and most of the people were killed. The Persian managed to escape with the help of the local villagers. As an expression of gratitude, he taught the villagers the art of weaving carpets.*

The weaving in this area is done in small villages by men and small boys, while women and girls perform the duties of spinning the wool. Quite often the weavers own one or two looms, which are set up for weaving in their homes rather than being centrally located in, and owned by, a factory; under these conditions carpet-weaving is known as a "cottage industry." A weaver will generally work an eight-hour day, tying from six thousand to twelve thousand knots, depending on the difficulty of the design.

Most of the carpet-weaving of this district is performed on order. Oriental rug merchants and importers will contract with an Indian firm for a specified number of carpets in a particular design, color, and quality. These are referred to in the trade as "contract goods."

When orders are received, the Indian broker or exporter (known as a "manufacturer") will make the necessary arrangements with a master weaver. This weaver, called a *dukandar*, will be issued the *naksha* (design

---

* Pande Cameron & Co., *A Note on the Hand-Knotted Carpet Industry in India* (mimeo, n.d.), p. 1.

PLATE 6.1:
THE MAKING OF A NAKSHA

79

plan), cotton for the foundation (warp and weft threads), and a weighed amount of wool for the pile. The *dukandar* may own several looms and will hire other weavers (called *bunkers*) to do the work at his or their own looms. The *dukandar* is responsible for inspecting the work of the *bunkers* and for transporting the carpets back to the broker when completed. The rug is then carefully inspected again and weighed to see that the proper amount of wool was used. The prenegotiated price for each carpet is paid, and the *dukandar* is given a commission which depends on the quality of workmanship.*

The broker is responsible for the finishing stages of the carpet's production. The carpet may be "carved"; borders and motifs are accentuated by the selective trimming to impart a three-dimensional effect (see Plate 6.3). All carpets are also trimmed to even the pile to the desired height. An exacting task, this trimming is still done by using long hand-shears. Some carpets are given a light chemical wash, in addition, to add more luster. The chemical-washing process is done by hand. Rugs washed in the United States and Europe generally have a more even luster than those washed in India.

---

* *Ibid.*, p. 2.

PLATE 6.2: *WOOL BEING WEIGHED BEFORE BEING ISSUED TO THE WEAVER*

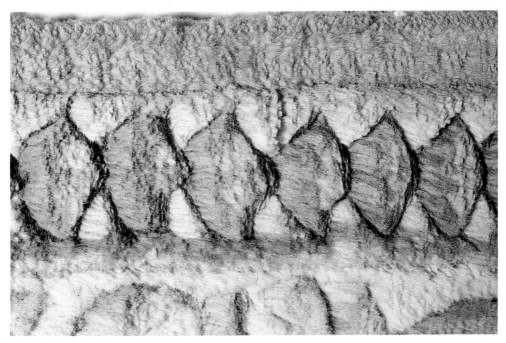

PLATE 6.3: *CARVED PILE OF AN INDIAN CARPET*

MIRZAPUR-BHADOHI *(Uttar Pradesh)*

The carpets of the Mirzapur-Bhadohi area are woven with a Persian knot on a cotton foundation. The weavers of this area are capable of producing carpets of medium-fine to medium-low qualities. The best-quality carpets usually are woven in Bhadohi and the lowest quality come from Mirzapur. The quality or coarseness of the weave depends largely on the quantity ordered. The majority of carpets woven in this area are "contract" or commercial goods—numerous carpets woven with the same design, in varying color combinations, sizes, and quality grades.

Three major types of designs are woven in the Mirzapur-Bhadohi area: French Savonnerie (Aubusson), Chinese, and Persian. To denote their Indian origin, these patterns are or should be prefixed with *Indo,* for example, Indo-Savonnerie or Indo-Tabriz (Persian).

French Savonnerie–type rugs are woven in pastel shades of rose, blue, green, and beige. These rugs have floral designs that are reminiscent of the French Savonnerie and Aubusson rugs of the seventeenth century. Most often the Indo-Savonnerie carpet has a floral medallion (see Plate 6.6), although it may be omitted; the empty field is surrounded by an elaborate floral border. The borders as well as the motifs in the field are accentuated by carving the pile (see Plate 6.3).

PLATE 6.4: *FINE-QUALITY INDO-PERSIAN, 6 ft. by 9 ft.,*
Courtesy of Pande Cameron Co.

PLATE 6.5: *FINE-QUALITY INDO-PERSIAN, 6 ft. by 9 ft.,*
Courtesy of Pande Cameron Co.

Indo-Chinese rugs usually have a central medallion, which may be either floral or *shou*-sign (see Plates 6.7 and 6.8). A variety of small Chinese motifs are scattered throughout the field. The designs and motifs are also carved.

Indian weavers are adept at copying the designs of all Persian carpets. Indo-Persian rugs appear in almost every Persian design. For example, Indo-Tabriz rugs are woven with a Hunting design (see Plate 6.9), as well as the

Medallion design (see Plate 6.10). Indo-Sarouk, Indo-Karaja (see Plate 6.11), Indo-Herez (see Plate 6.12), Indo-Kashan (see Plate 6.13), and many other Persian designs, as well as adaptations of traditional designs, are all woven to order in a range of qualities.

Importers will stock rugs of varying qualities from the Mirzapur-Bhadohi area. Many different designs are often available in a specific-quality grade. Each importer will identify and label each quality grade with

PLATE 6.8:
INDO-CHINESE
3 ft. 1 in. by 5 ft. 1 in.
Courtesy of Mr. and
Mrs. John Ficzeri

86

PLATE 6.9:
INDO-TABRIZ
(Hunting Design)
4 ft. by 6 ft.
Courtesy of Alfandari
and Etessami Co., Inc.

his own trademarked name. It is impossible to rely upon these names or trademarks to differentiate quality among rugs from different importers.

When comparing rugs from different importers, the buyer must base his evaluation on a direct analysis of the two rugs. Count the number of knots per square inch or centimeter. In comparing carpets of the same age and weaving center, higher knot counts usually mean better-quality rugs. The clarity of the design is important; the finer the knotting, the clearer the design. The fringe should be examined; the fringe is an extension of the warp threads. The finer or thinner the fringe, the finer and tighter the knots. A thick fringe will have thick, coarse knots; the pile will therefore be much less dense than with a more finely knotted rug.

PLATE 6.10:
INDO-TABRIZ
(Medallion Design)
3 ft. by 5 ft.
Courtesy of Alfandari
and Etessami Co., Inc.

PLATE 6.11:
INDO-KARAJA
2 ft. by 4 ft.
Courtesy of Mr. and
Mrs. Howard Smith

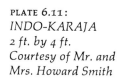

88

PLATE 6.12: *INDO-HEREZ*
3 ft. by 5 ft.
Courtesy of Alfandari
and Etessami Co., Inc.

PLATE 6.13: *INDO-KASHAN*
3 ft. by 5 ft.
Courtesy of Alfandari
and Etessami Co., Inc.

PLATE 6.14: *INDO-PERSIAN, 6 ft. by 9 ft., Courtesy of Pande Cameron Co.*

AGRA *(Uttar Pradesh)*

KNOT: *Persian*
WARP: *cotton*
WEFT: *cotton*
PILE: *good-quality wool; short in length*
FRINGE: *small, tightly woven* kelim *with knotted fringe at both ends*
SELVEDGE: *overcast with wool*

The ancient town of Agra is located approximately 125 miles southeast of Delhi. The magnificent Taj Mahal was built here by Shah Jehan in 1648.

The Moghul emperor, Akbar the Great, introduced carpet-weaving in Agra when he established his capital there more than four hundred years ago. The weaving of carpets has continued in spite of several severe recessions in the industry. The majority of rugs are woven in factories. Currently, the total number of carpets made in Agra is relatively small in comparison to that of the eastern districts of Uttar Pradesh.

The rugs of Agra are tightly woven on a cotton foundation; the pile is trimmed quite short. They are generally of fine quality; however, the quality does vary. The majority of Agra rugs are woven in smaller sizes.

The designs most often woven are adaptations of those from Persian (see Plate 6.15) and Turkoman carpets. Kashan and Isfahan are the most popular of the Persian designs woven; a Tekke-type *gul* is the Turkoman design most often used.

JAIPUR *(Rajasthan)*

KNOT: *Persian*
WARP: *cotton*
WEFT: *cotton; single or double*
PILE: *good-quality wool; medium to medium-short in length*
FRINGE: *tightly woven* kelim *usually with a narrow, colored strip; knotted fringe at both ends*
SELVEDGE: *overcast with wool*

The province of Rajasthan is one of India's largest-volume wool-producing areas. The wool from this area is of good quality and withstands wear quite well. Rajasthan's weaving industry is located in and around the city of Jaipur. Carpets have been woven in Jaipur since the Moghul emperors established workshops there more than four hundred years ago.

Rugs woven in Jaipur are finely woven on a cotton foundation. They

PLATE 6.15: *AGRA*
3 ft. 2 in. by 5 ft. 10 in.
Courtesy of Dr. and
Mrs. Robert Fulmer

may be woven with either a single or double weft. The single-wefted rugs are more finely woven with a slightly shorter pile than those woven with a double weft. In appearance, the back of the Jaipur carpets resembles those of the rugs of Pakistan (see Plate 7.2).

The wool used for the pile is of excellent quality; local wool is usually blended with wool imported from New Zealand. The New Zealand wool is stronger and more lustrous and gives the carpet a finer sheen.

The designs are generally quite intricate. Commonly woven designs are adaptations of the Turkish Ghiordes Prayer (see Plate 6.16), a Tekke-type Turkoman *gul* (see Plate 6.17), and Caucasian designs and motifs (see Plate 6.18).

PLATE 6.16: *JAIPUR (Prayer Design), 2 ft. 7 in. by 4 ft. 6 in.,*
Courtesy of Miss Polly Price

PLATE 6.17: *JAIPUR (Bukhara)*
2 ft. 8 in. by 4 ft. 2 in., Courtesy of Miss Polly Price

PLATE 6.18:
JAIPUR
(Shirvan Design)
2 ft. by 4 ft.
Courtesy of
Kapoor Carpets

KASHMIR

KNOT: *Persian*
WARP: *cotton; silk*
WEFT: *cotton; silk*
PILE: *good-quality wool, short; silk*
FRINGE: *small* kelim *with knotted fringe*
SELVEDGE: *overcast with wool or silk*
(same material as the pile)

Kashmir, India's northernmost province, did not officially become part of India until 1957. It had previously been an independent state ruled by maharajas. Since the early fifteenth century, Kashmir has enjoyed a reputation for weaving fine carpets. Most of the weaving in Kashmir is located in Srinagar and its surrounding areas.

The weavers of Kashmir are experts at copying the designs of the finest-quality Persian carpets. Copies of antique Kashan Prayer and

PLATE 6.19: *KASHMIR*
4 ft. by 6 ft.
Courtesy of Mori S.A.

Medallion-design rugs (see Plate 6.19) are beautifully executed. Excellent copies of Turkish and Turkoman rugs are also woven (see Plate 6.20).

Kashmiri rugs are usually woven with wool pile on a cotton foundation; however all-silk rugs are also woven. The wool and silk used are from Kashmir and are generally of excellent quality.

The amount of carpets produced in Kashmir is relatively small in comparison to that of the Mirzapur-Bhadohi area. The few rugs exported from Kashmir to the United States are usually in small sizes. The majority of Kashmir rugs are imported by the European markets, and these sizes may range from small to rather large room-sized carpets.

Rugs woven in Kashmir are usually of excellent quality; however, careful inspection of Kashmiri rugs is necessary, especially when purchasing the rug in Kashmir or in other parts of India (see p. 78). Not all rugs are woven in supervised weaving centers; many are woven by individuals in their homes. Consequently, there is a wide range in the quality of workmanship. Imperfections may occur in the knotting, designs may be poorly executed, wool or silk may be trimmed unevenly, or the rugs even may be washed poorly. For example, although the rug may be finely knotted, the design may have been poorly executed, and have objectionable irregularities or other mistakes.

A chain-stitched rug that is similar to crewel work is also made in Kashmir, and is called the "Jewel of Kashmir." These rugs are not genuine Oriental rugs; they are not hand-knotted. They are meant for decorative purposes only, for they do not withstand wear very well.

7

The Rugs of Pakistan

PAKISTAN SHARES India's four-hundred-year history of carpet-weaving. The Moghul emperors established carpet-weaving workshops in Lahore and Multan in the sixteenth century. In 1600, the East India Carpet Company was founded in Lahore by British merchants for the express purpose of weaving Oriental rugs.

In 1947 the British granted independence to the Indian subcontinent. At that time, what is now Pakistan was created from the northwest areas

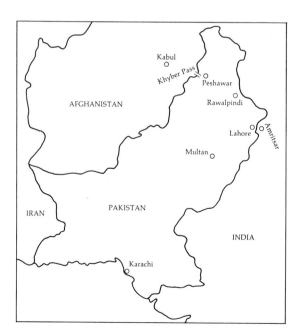

FIGURE 7-A: *PAKISTAN*

of India. Religion was the major factor in the partitioning, Pakistan being Moslem and India being Hindu. After the partition, many Moslem weavers moved from India to Lahore and other parts of Pakistan. These weavers were the foundation of a revitalized rug-weaving industry in the new country of Pakistan.

The infant government recognized the need for industry and employment. Government subsidies to the early Pakistani carpet-weaving industry made the prices of their rugs very competitive in foreign markets. Pakistan soon emerged as one of the world's leading manufacturers of handmade Oriental rugs.

STRUCTURAL CHARACTERISTICS

KNOT: *Persian*
WARP: *cotton*
WEFT: *cotton*
PILE: *wool with a lustrous appearance; short to medium-short in length*
FRINGE: *small kelim with knotted fringe at both ends*
SELVEDGE: *overcast with wool*

Pakistani carpets are finely knotted, yielding designs that are crisp and well defined. The Persian knot is used with a cotton foundation.

The weavers are able to change from one type of weave to another by changing the extent to which the warp threads are depressed when the knots are tied (see Plate 2.1). The more depressed the warp threads, the thicker the body of the carpet is and the more knots that can be tied in a horizontal inch.

The two types of weave used in Pakistani rugs are referred to as the Mori and Persian weaves. In both types of weaves the quality of the rug is expressed by a set of numbers, for example, 9/16 or 11/22. The first number is the number of horizontal knots in a linear inch; the second number is the number of vertical knots in a linear inch. The number of knots per square inch can easily be computed by multiplying the two numbers together; a 9/16 rug will have 144 knots per square inch and an 11/22 rug will have 264 knots per square inch.

The Persian weave used in rugs of Persian design gives an appearance quite similar to the back of the Persian carpets (see Plate 7.1). Persian rugs will have approximately the same number of knots in a horizontal inch as in a vertical inch. Single-ply Persian knots are tied on the depressed warp threads. The number of horizontal knots (or rows of knots) per linear inch is slightly less than the number of vertical knots (or rows of knots) per

PLATE 7.1: *PERSIAN WEAVE. Because of the warp thread depression, only one loop of each knot is visible on the back of the rug.*

PLATE 7.2: *MORI WEAVE. Because the warp threads are on the same level, both loops of a knot are visible on the back of the rug.*

linear inch. The quality ranges from 13/15 to 18/20, with intermediate grades of 14/16 and 16/18.

The Mori weave characteristically is woven in the "Bukhara" design rugs from Pakistan (see Plate 7.2). Persian knots, which may be either single- or double-ply, are tied on warp threads that are on the same level (not depressed). In this type of weave, the quality of the double-ply rugs will range from 8/12 to 8/18, with intermediate grades of 8/14, 9/14, and 9/16; the single-ply rugs quality ranges from 10/20 to 12/24, with intermediate grades of 11/22, 11/24, and 12/22. When counting the knots of a Mori weave, one often makes the mistake of counting the same knot twice. When knots are tied on warp threads on the same level, each knot will have two loops clearly visible.

The pile of most Pakistani rugs is a good-quality wool from local sheep. Better-quality rugs use a blend of local wool and wool imported from Australia. Australian wool contains more lanolin and is a stronger wool that yields a more durable and lustrous carpet. Pakistani rugs are noted for their rich sheen. This is due largely to the chemical or luster wash given before export.

DESIGNS

All designs woven in Pakistani rugs have been adopted or adapted from other weaving centers. The "Bukhara" design was adopted from the rugs of the Turkoman Tekke tribe. Designs from other Turkoman tribes, as well as many others from the weaving centers of Turkey, Iran, and the Caucasus, are also woven. These will be discussed in the following sections.

Turkoman

Of the numerous types of designs woven in Pakistan, the "Bukhara" is the most popular and widely known. This design is a Repeated *Gul* motif (see Plates 7.3 and 7.4). *Guls* are small rectilinear emblems which were once unique to the Turkoman tribes that wove them. The Yomud, Salor, Sariq, and Tekke are the Turkoman *guls* that are most often woven in Pakistan (see Plate 7.5).

PLATE 7.3: *BUKHARA*
3 ft. 1 in. by 5 ft. 2 in.

PLATE 7.4: *BUKHARA*
2 ft. 1 in. by 3 ft. 2 in.
Courtesy of Dr. and Mrs. Robert Hurd

PLATE 7.5: *BUKHARA BAG FACE*
2 ft. by 3 ft.
Courtesy of Miss Mia Brickley

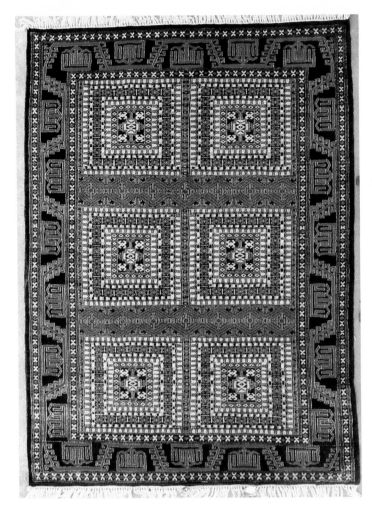

The *Hatchlou* is another Turkoman design which has been adopted and adapted by the weavers of Pakistan. The field of the *Hatchlou* design has been divided into quadrants or sections by perpendicular bars or stripes (see Plate 7.6).

Other Turkoman weavings also have been adopted. Among these are the various bag faces and tent hangings (see Plate 7.5). Turkoman tribes had many different sizes of bags for a variety of uses. Each bag normally had a back that was woven, a *kelim* or flat weave, and a front surface ("face") of knotted pile. Turkoman bags are often used as carpets after the *kelim* backing has been removed. Pakistani ("Bukhara") bag faces are copies of the Turkoman tribal bags.

The use of colors in Turkoman-design rugs is rather limited; only two or three colors generally are used. A red or rust ground with navy blue or black motifs and borders is the most common color scheme; cream, camel, blue, and ivory are also used as ground colors.

Turkey

The Ghiordes Prayer design originated in Turkey and was one of the first designs woven in Pakistani rugs. On either side of the field, columns extend upward to support the *spandrels* on either side of the *mihrab*, or prayer arch. From the arch or niche a small lamp is suspended and at the base of the columns is centered a vase of flowers (see Plate 7.7).

The *Saff* (family prayer rug) also employs the *mihrab*, or prayer arch; multiple *mihrabs* are placed side by side. The number of *mihrabs* in a *Saff* may range from two to as many as nine, with each being a different color (see Plate 7.8).

PLATE 7.7:
GHIORDES PRAYER DESIGN
2 ft. 5 in. by 4 ft. 1 in.

PLATE 7.8: *SAFF DESIGN, 3 ft. by 7 ft.*

Iran

A wide variety of Persian designs are woven. Common designs derived from Persian rugs include Medallion designs resembling those of Tabriz and Kashan (see Plates 7.9 and 7.10); Prayer rugs from Kashan; and all-over Shah Abbas designs from Tabriz, Kashan, and Isfahan (see Plate 7.11). Finely executed Picture carpets are woven which depict biblical stories and Persian or Moghul legends.

Caucasus

The brilliant colors and the bold geometric designs of the Caucasian rugs are woven in the rugs of Pakistan. The designs traditionally associated with Kazakh, Shirvan, and Kuba are the most frequently copied. These Pakistani copies are often more finely woven than their genuine Caucasian counterparts (see Plate 7.12).

WEAVING CENTERS

Hand-knotted carpets are woven throughout Pakistan in numerous small villages. The greatest concentration of these is around Lahore, Karachi, and Peshawar (see Figure 7-A).

Lahore and the Punjab province

Carpets were hand-woven in Lahore as early as the fifteenth century. In 1600, the East India Carpet Company was founded there.

PLATE 7.9: *KASHAN DESIGN, 3 ft. 1 in. by 4 ft. 11 in.*
Courtesy of Alfandari and Etessami Co., Inc.

PLATE 7.10: *HUNTING DESIGN*, *3 ft. by 5 ft., Courtesy of Beco Carpets*

PLATE 7.11:
KASHAN DESIGN
4 ft. 2 in.
by 5 ft. 11 in.
Courtesy of
Alfandari and
Etessami Co., Inc.

Approximately 85 percent of the total number of carpets woven in Pakistan are made in small weaving areas scattered throughout the Punjab province. Much of the weaving here is done in small factories and in the homes of weavers.

The variety of designs woven in this area is immense. Turkoman, Persian, Turkish, and Caucasian designs are all used. The type of weave used also varies; Persian-design rugs are woven with the Persian weave and the other designs are generally woven with the Mori weave.

Karachi

Karachi is one of the largest weaving centers in Pakistan. The rugs of this area are finely woven with short pile, which gives these carpets clearly defined designs and motifs. A variety of designs are woven, but the most common are those adapted from the Turkoman tribes. The Mori weave is generally woven in both single- and double-ply.

The majority of rugs are woven in small sizes; however some larger rugs are also woven.

Peshawar

A variety of designs are woven in the Peshawar area. The quality of workmanship is generally not as fine as that of Lahore and Karachi.

PLATE 7.12:
SHIRVAN DESIGN
4 ft. 1 in. by 6 ft. 4 in.
Courtesy of Alfandari
and Etessami Co., Inc.

109

8

The Rugs
of Romania

FOR MORE THAN three hundred years the art of weaving Oriental carpets
has been practiced in Romania. The structure and design of the early
Romanian carpets were strongly influenced by the Ottoman Turks, who
occupied Romania from 1526 to 1699. By the beginning of the twentieth
century, the weaving of Oriental rugs was well established in the towns of
Brăila, Iaşi, Galaţi, Cluj, Făgăras, and Bucharest.

HISTORICAL PERSPECTIVE

Early carpet production was rather limited, but these carpets were of excellent quality. Designs were adopted from those of the ancient Turkish
and Caucasian weaving centers. The Tuduc workshop, in particular, became
famous for its excellent reproductions of classical Caucasian and Turkish
carpets. Made in the early part of the twentieth century, these reproductions
were so well done that in 1933 the Victoria and Albert Museum purchased
what was believed to be a seventeenth-century Ushak. This rug later was
found to be a Tuduc copy. In a similar situation in the late 1950s, the
Berlin Museum purchased a carpet that was also discovered to be another
Ushak copy from the Tuduc workshop.

After World War I, many Armenians immigrated to Romania and
other Balkan countries. Many of these immigrants were expert weavers
and established workshops for the weaving of Oriental carpets. One such
workshop in Brăila was reported to have had over three hundred weavers
between 1925 and 1930.

CURRENT CARPET PRODUCTION

Since the early 1950s carpet-weaving in Romania has become standardized. A network of handicraft cooperatives scattered throughout Romania has been set up. Their activities are guided and coordinated by the Central Board of the Folk Art and Artistic Handicrafts of the Central Union of Handicrafts Cooperative (UCECOM). Women do most of the weaving in these cooperatives, and in smaller workshops. In some areas, rugs are woven by individuals in their homes; a small number of rugs are woven in workshops set up in monasteries or convents.

Until 1975, the majority of Romanian rugs went to Europe. At that time the United States Government negotiated new trade agreements in which Romania was granted Favored Nation Status; the import duty on Romanian rugs was dropped from 45 percent to 11 percent. Romanian rugs have become increasingly available on the American market.

The majority of Oriental rugs woven in Romania are made under contract with rug importers and wholesalers. The contract is made for a designated amount of carpeting to be delivered within a certain amount of time. Designs, color combinations, sizes, and qualities are specified by the importer. Special requests for adaptations in designs and color combinations are regularly taken.

FIGURE 8-A: *ROMANIA*

There are no unique or traditional designs associated with Romanian Oriental rugs. For several hundred years the designs woven in Romania have been designs adopted and adapted from the weaving centers of the Caucasus, Persia, and Turkey. For this reason, Oriental rugs from Romania take their names from the design or type of rug that has been copied. An example is the Romanian Tabriz or Tabriz-design rug made in Romania. Currently, cartoons of more than five hundred different designs and adaptations of the traditional designs of the major weaving centers can be woven. In some instances, the designs of the Romanian rugs are better executed than in the original rug.

STRUCTURE

The most distinguishing structural feature of Romanian carpets is the uniform appearance of the carpet back (see Plate 8.2). The variations in knot sizes, which are normally encountered in hand-knotted Oriental rugs,

PLATE 8.1: *THE WEAVING OF A ROMANIAN CARPET*

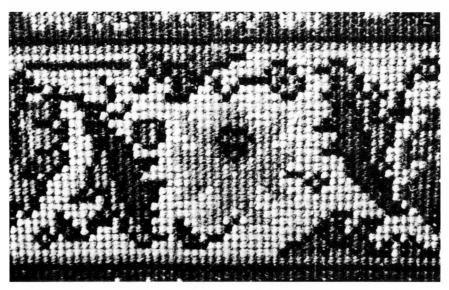

PLATE 8.2: *THE BACK OF A BUCHARESTI-QUALITY ROMANIAN CARPET.*
Note the uniform appearance and the regularity of the knots.

are so slight that the carpet back seems almost machine-made in appearance. This is due in part to the looms, which have been well engineered and allow an even tension to be maintained during the weaving process. The shape of Romanian carpets also tends to be more regular than those carpets woven on a more primitive or nomadic loom.

The wool used for the pile comes from Romanian sheep. It has been machine spun and is of good quality. Chrome dyes are used, with a wide range of rich, mellow colors. The dyes are colorfast and will not fade when washed or exposed to sunlight. All sizes of carpets are woven; standard sizes range from small 90 by 150 centimeters (3 by 5 feet) to room-size carpets. Larger sizes, as well as round rugs and runners, are also available.

After the carpet has been woven, it is taken from the loom for a final trimming to even the pile, and then washed. The larger cooperatives have their own facilities for doing this; the smaller ones send their carpets to the large establishments in Bucharest. All Romanian rugs receive a light chemical wash before export; this in no way harms the carpet and actually enriches its appearance. After export from Romania, some rugs are given a heavy chemical wash to give the carpet an antique appearance.

The quality of Romanian rugs is determined primarily by the knot count, unlike Persian carpets, which have so many variables (quality of wool, execution of design, and weaving characteristics) complicating the knot-count-to-quality relationship. Quality is standardized into several distinct grades based on knot count (number of knots per square meter). The quality grades range from 40,000 knots per square meter (25 knots per square inch) to 300,000 knots per square meter (194 knots per square inch).

When exported, all Romanian rugs are labeled with a tag denoting quality. If this tag is not present at the time of purchase, it is quite easy to determine the quality by simply counting the number of knots per square inch.

QUALITY GRADES

Even though the names of quality grades are also names of towns or areas, there is no relationship between the two. Bucharest quality rugs, for example, are woven throughout Romania—even in the cooperatives in Brăila and Braşov.

There are two types of hand-knotted carpets woven in Romania today: those with wool pile and a cotton foundation and those with wool pile and a woolen foundation (see Figure 8-B).

Cotton Foundation

DORNA

The least expensive and lowest in quality of all Romanian hand-knotted carpets is the Dorna. These rugs are woven on a cotton foundation with a knot count of 40,000 knots per square meter (25 knots per square inch). See Plate 8.3.

	QUALITY GRADE	KNOTS PER SQ. METER	KNOTS PER SQ. INCH
COTTON	Dorna	40,000	25
FOUNDATION	Bucharesti	110,000	70
	Brăila	160,000	103
	Mureş	200,000	129
	Olt	250,000	160
	Milcov	300,000	194
WOOLEN	Bran	92,400	60
FOUNDATION	Transylvania	121,600	79
	Braşov	160,000	103
	Harmon	200,000	129
	Postavarul	240,000	155

FIGURE 8-B: *QUALITY GRADES OF ROMANIAN CARPETS*

PLATE 8.3: *DORNA QUALITY*
6 ft. by 9 ft.

BUCHARESTI

Virtually all sizes and types of designs are woven in this quality. Bucharesti quality rugs make up 90 percent of all Romanian rugs on the American market and 70 percent of all Romanian rugs available on European markets. With a knot count of 110,000 knots per square meter (70 knots per square inch), these rugs can provide an inexpensive, serviceable floor covering. They wear as well as or better than any other rug with a comparable knot count. See Plates 8.4 and 8.5.

BRAILA

With a knot count of 160,000 knots per square meter (103 knots per square inch), the Braila is the intermediate grade of Romanian carpets woven with a cotton foundation. As with the Bucharesti quality, virtually all sizes and shapes are woven. The most common designs are the Shah Abbas, Medallion, Boteh, and Prayer; these have been adopted from Persian weaving centers, notably those of Kashan, Qum, Tabriz, and Sarouk. See Plate 8.6.

MURES

A excellent-quality rug, Mures is woven with cotton warp and weft threads. The designs commonly woven are adaptations of traditional Persian patterns from the weaving centers of Sarouk, Tabriz, Kashan, Herez, and Mashad. Sizes range from 170 by 240 centimeters (approximately 6 by 9 feet) to larger room-size rugs. The knot count is 200,000 knots per square meter (129 knots per square inch). See Plate 8.7.

OLT

With a knot count of 250,000 knots per square meter (160 knots per square inch), the Olt is one of the best Romanian rugs made. A design reminiscent of old French tapestries is one of the most common designs. Designs from the weaving centers of Iran and Turkey are also woven. See Plates 8.8 and 8.9.

PLATE 8.4:
BUCHARESTI QUALITY
2 ft. 7 in. by 4 ft. 7 in.
Courtesy of Mr. and Mrs.
Robert Scharlotte

opposite,
PLATE 8.5:
BUCHARESTI QUALITY
3 ft. by 5 ft.
Courtesy of Mr. and
Mrs. Louis Bickey

117

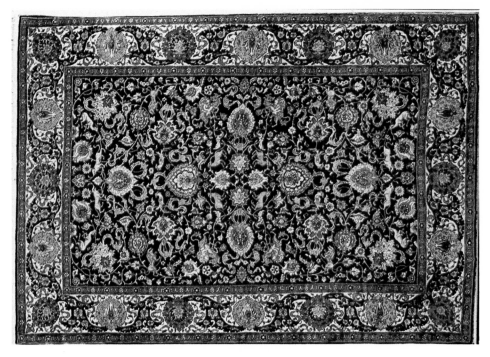

PLATE 8.6: *BRAILA QUALITY*
6 ft. by 9 ft.

PLATE 8.7: *MURES QUALITY*
6 ft. by 9 ft.
Courtesy of Kelaty Rug Corp.

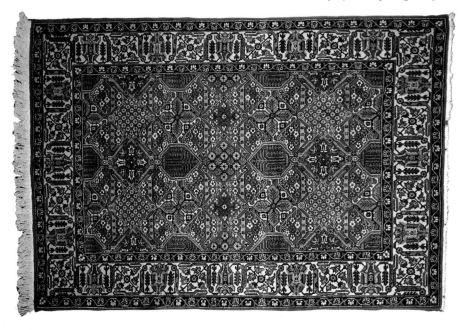

MILCOV

The finest-quality carpet woven in Romania is the Milcov. Designs are beautifully executed copies of the finest-quality Persian rugs. They are woven on a cotton foundation, with a knot count of 300,000 knots per square meter (194 knots per square inch).

Woolen Foundation

BRAN

With a knot count of 92,400 knots per square meter (60 knots per square inch), the Bran is the least expensive of the Romanian rugs woven

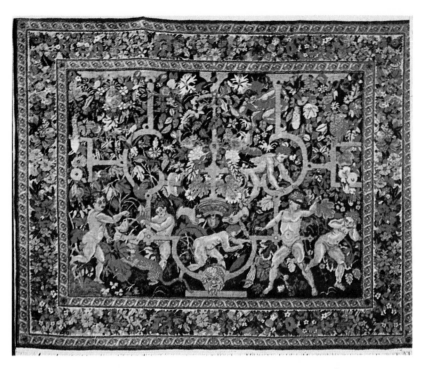

PLATE 8.9:
OLT QUALITY
4 ft. by 6 ft.

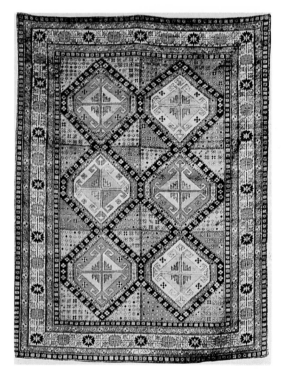

PLATE 8.10:
BRAN QUALITY
6 ft. by 8 ft.

PLATE 8.11: *TRANSYLVANIA QUALITY*, *3 ft. 3 in. by 5 ft.*

on a woolen foundation. Designs from Turkey and the Caucasus are those most often woven. See Plate 8.10.

TRANSYLVANIA

The Transylvania quality is a good durable rug woven on a foundation of wool warp and weft threads. These rugs are generally small, with sizes ranging from 100 by 150 centimeters to 170 by 260 centimeters (approximately 3 by 5 feet to 6 by 9 feet). The knot count is 121,600 knots per square meter (79 knots per square inch). The colors and designs used are beautifully executed copies of those traditionally associated with the weaving centers of Turkey and the Caucasus. See Plates 8.11 and 8.12.

BRASOV

Many of the designs woven in the rugs of Braşov quality are copied from those found in older Turkish rugs. These rugs are a very good quality and are woven with wool warp and weft threads. The knot count is 160,000 knots per square meter (103 knots per square inch). In this quality, rug sizes are generally 120 by 170 centimeters (4 by 6 feet) or slightly larger. See Plate 8.13.

PLATE 8.12:
TRANSLVANIA QUALITY
4 ft. 5 in. by 7 ft.
Courtesy of Kelaty Rug Corp.

PLATE 8.13:
BRASOV QUALITY
4 ft. by 7 ft.

HARMON

Designs woven in this excellent-quality carpet are beautifully executed copies of traditional Persian designs. These carpets are woven on a woolen foundation with a knot count of 200,000 knots per square meter (129 knots per square inch). Common sizes are 200 by 300 centimeters (6 by 9 feet) or larger.

POSTAVARUL

The finest-quality Romanian carpet woven on a woolen foundation is the Postavarul. These excellent-quality carpets are finely woven with crisp designs. The knot count is 240,000 knots per square meter (155 knots per square inch).

9

Pileless Carpets: Dhurries and Kelims

DHURRIES AND KELIMS, sometimes called flat weaves, are the oldest and most widespread form of handmade carpets. They have been woven for several thousand years, although their origins have been lost in antiquity. The scope of our discussion of these pileless carpets is limited to those woven in India, Pakistan, Tibet, and Romania.

A renewed interest in primitive and folk art has brought an awareness and appreciation of the simple, bold designs of *kelims* and *dhurries*. They present an attractive alternative to the more expensive hand-knotted pile carpets.

Dhurries and *kelims* are hand-woven on a loom in much the same manner as hand-knotted pile carpets. *Kelims* are woven of wool. *Dhurries* were originally woven of cotton, but since the end of World War II they have been made of wool also. Occasionally other materials are used, such as jute, silk, or a combination of wool and cotton. There are no fundamental differences in the construction of *dhurries* and *kelims*; the primary difference is in materials used and where they are woven.

Designs are formed by colored weft threads which are woven back and forth through the warp threads (see Figure 9-A). A variation in the weaving of pileless carpets lies in the treatment of the point at which two different colors of weft threads meet. The threads may be kept separate, creating a slit at the juncture, or joined by the sharing of a common warp thread.

Slit Weave. Small slits in the weave occur as each colored weft thread is woven back on itself to complete its own colored area of the design.

Shared Warp. As two weft threads of different colors meet, they turn back upon themselves at a common or shared warp thread. There is no slit between two colors in this type of weave.

In determining the quality of a pileless rug, there are several points to be considered:

1. The rug should be tightly woven; the tightness of weave should be uniform throughout the carpet. Generally speaking, the tighter the weave and the thinner the carpet, the better the quality. This comes from the use of finer-spun thread or yarn, which allows a tighter weave and more intricate designs.

2. The designs should be well executed, being aesthetically pleasing in their proportions and choice of colors.

3. The wool should be of good quality, finely combed and well spun. Rugs which are "fuzzy" or "frizzy" have not been well spun, and may include foreign matter.

4. The dyes should be colorfast. There should be no fading or running of colors when wet.

5. Some irregularities in the shape of a carpet are to be expected. Noticeably misshaped rugs and rugs that do not lie flat or that bow should be avoided. Some slight rippling is to be expected in pileless carpets, however.

A pileless carpet should not be expected to withstand heavy use as well as a good-quality pile carpet. The thick, tightly woven pile of a knotted carpet serves as a cushion to constant wear. A pileless carpet will, however, wear well if given proper care.

Proper care will greatly prolong the life span of a *dhurrie* or *kelim*. The rug should be reversed two to three times a year and turned over about twice a year. This allows the *kelim* or *dhurrie* to wear evenly. A good-

FIGURE 9-A: *KELIM WEAVES*

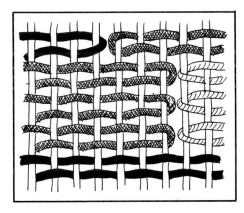

Slit Weave

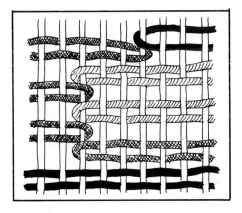

Shared Warp

quality pileless carpet, properly cared for, may be expected to last seventy-five to a hundred years. Many *kelims* and *dhurries* are still in excellent condition although their age may exceed 150 years.

A padding should be used under a *kelim* or *dhurrie*. The pad should be thin, about one-eighth inch thick. This helps prevent the rug from slipping yet preserves the natural state of the *kelim* or *dhurrie*.

DHURRIES

Dhurries are reversible pileless carpets which may be woven of wool or cotton. Currently they are woven in India and Pakistan. Ninety percent of the *dhurries* available on the European and American markets are woven in India. The remaining 10 percent are woven in Pakistan.

"Tibetan" Dhurries

In the past, beautiful *dhurries* were woven in an area between Kashmir and Tibet; these pileless carpets became known as "Tibetan" *dhurries*. Most of these *dhurries* are now woven by Tibetans who reside in northern Pakistan and India.

The "Tibetan" *dhurries* often have Medallion-type designs with small geometric motifs in the field (see Plate 9.1). The colors are usually subdued shades of camel, golden yellow, and brown.

Indian Dhurries

Dhurries are woven throughout India. The Bhadohi area is responsible for the largest volume as well as the finest-quality woolen *dhurries*. The finest-quality cotton *dhurries* are woven in Srinagar and Agra. In some of the Agra carpets, silk and gold metallic threads are used to highlight and accent the designs.

A wide variety of designs and color combinations are woven in Indian *dhurries*. Some designs are reproductions and adaptations of antique designs, while others are new creations. The designs may be simple, such as multicolored bands or stripes, or more complex and elaborate Garden-type designs with trees and animal figures (see Plates 9.3, 9.4, and 9.5). Small repeated geometric motifs are also commonly used (see Plate 9.6). The colors may range from bold vibrant reds and blues to more mellow pastel hues.

PLATE 9.1: *TIBETAN DHURRIE, 6 ft. by 9 ft., Courtesy of Stark Carpet Co.*

PLATE 9.2:
INDIAN DHURRIE
5 ft. 3 in. by 7 ft. 4 in.
Courtesy of Mr. and
Mrs. Kenneth Kangas

PLATE 9.3:
INDIAN DHURRIE
6 ft. by 9 ft.
Courtesy of Pande Cameron Co.

PLATE 9.4: *INDIAN DHURRIE, 6 ft. by 9 ft., Courtesy of Pande Cameron Co.*

PLATE 9.5: *INDIAN DHURRIE, 6 ft. by 8 ft., Courtesy of Stark Carpet Co.*

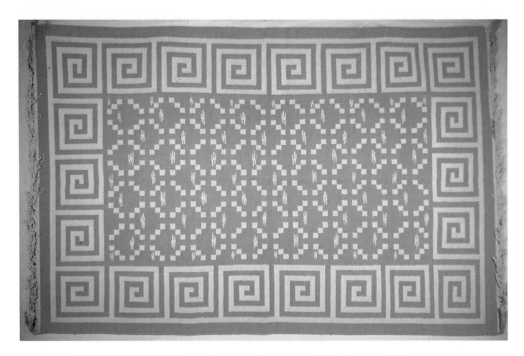

PLATE 9.6: *INDIAN DHURRIE, 6 ft. by 9 ft., Courtesy of Mrs. Peggy Robinson*

PLATE 9.7: *WALL-HANGING,*
woven in India with Kelim technique
Courtesy of Mr. Russell Herbert

Some *dhurries* are woven with no fringe. Instead a narrow woven strip, at the bottom and top of the rugs, is turned under and overcast in such a way that the rug is still reversible. Virtually all sizes are woven, from small mats to large room-size rugs. Decorative pieces are also woven (see Plate 9.7).

ROMANIAN KELIMS

The pileless carpets or *kelims* of Romania are referred to as *scoarta*. Romanian *kelims* are woven with the slit-weave or shared-warp technique. The slit-weave technique is used in the finer-quality rugs. In both types of weave, the front is the same as the back, yielding carpets that are reversible.

Both *kelims* and pile carpets have been woven in Romania for hundreds of years. Romanian *kelims* are colorful examples of their folk art. Many of their designs still retain the tradition and character of the area in which they were originally woven. Modern adaptations of traditional designs as well as new creations are also woven. Over four thousand weavers, both in individual homes and government cooperatives scattered throughout Romania, are engaged in the weaving of *kelims* (see Plate 9.8).

Three areas of Romania are known for their rich history of weaving *kelims:* Moldavia, Transylvania, and Oltenia. Each area has its own unique designs and excellent weaves.

Moldavian *kelims* are woven in the handicraft cooperatives of Tg. Meamt, Iasi, and Radauti. Stripes are characteristic of Moldavian *kelims*. These stripes usually alternate with floral motifs and bands. The most common colors used in the Moldavian *kelims* are green, brown, gray, and black; the designs and motifs are generally cherry red, pink, or mauve.

Transylvanian *kelims* are very different in design from those of the hand-knotted pile carpets that are woven there. In the *kelims,* small geometric motifs are woven in stripes or in panels through the rug. Shades of brown, black, green, and red are commonly used.

Oltenian *kelims* are considered to be the finest of the Romanian *kelims*. They are currently being woven in the handicraft cooperatives in Tismana, Tg. Jiu, and Craiova. Oltenian designs are more floral in character than those of most *kelims,* their weavers having the special talent of weaving curved designs and motifs. Borders are given special attention; they carry out the theme and further complement the motifs in the central field. Traditional colors of cherry red, blue, black, white, and green are still used. The ground of the central field is usually dark-colored and quite often black (see Plate 9.9).

The range of *kelim* designs now woven has been expanded from its base of traditional Romanian folk designs to include designs based on those woven in hand-knotted carpets. Garden designs and nature scenes with

animal and bird figures are often woven, as well as Medallion designs with various small geometric motifs scattered throughout the field (see Plates 9.10 and 9.11). Small borders, similar to those of hand-knotted pile carpets, are often woven. There are a wide variety of color combinations available, ranging from earth tones to the brighter, more intense hues.

Romanian *kelims* are finely woven with excellent-quality wool. The majority of these *kelims* are now woven on cotton warp threads. A few rugs in small sizes are woven with natural-colored goat's hair. Romanian *kelims* are woven in a variety of sizes from small mats to room-size rugs.

OTHER PILELESS CARPETS

There are other pileless carpets woven in India that are handmade. Most of these are not hand-woven and are therefore not considered to be genuine Oriental rugs.

Namda

The *namda* is made of felt. The design may be appliquéd onto the felt or dyed wool pressed into the rug during the felting process. These are not considered to be genuine Oriental rugs, even though they are made in India.

PLATE 9.9: *ROMANIAN KELIM (Oltenia), 2 ft. by 4 ft.,*
Courtesy of Mr. Russell Herbert

Gabba

The *gabba* is a woolen fabric rug with designs that have been embroidered onto the wool. They are also made in India but are not genuine Oriental rugs.

Jewel of Kashmir

The Jewel of Kashmir is a chain-stitched rug made in Kashmir. Because they are stitched and not woven, they are not considered to be genuine Oriental rugs.

Drugget

A *drugget* is a pileless carpet, usually woven of cotton. They are coarsely woven and are usually made in small sizes. *Druggets* made in India are considered to be genuine Oriental rugs.

PLATE 9.10: *ROMANIAN KELIM*
6 ft. by 9 ft. 2 in.
Courtesy of Stark Carpet Co.

PLATE 9.11: *ROMANIAN KELIM*
6 ft. 2 in. by 9 ft. 2 in.
Courtesy of Stark Carpet Co.

© STARK CARPET CO.

© STARK CARPET CO.

10

Buying and Caring for an Oriental Rug

THERE ARE no hard-and-fast rules that govern the buying of an Oriental rug. The qualities that made each Oriental rug unique can also prove bewildering when one is confronted with a series of strange names, huge assortments of color combinations, and ranges of quality. Each rug must be evaluated on its own merits, considering its condition, size, design, price, and country of origin.

Established and reputable Oriental-rug dealers can be a tremendous help. They usually have a large selection of rugs from which to choose. They also should be able to advise you on the wearing qualities, investment potential, and care of your Oriental rug. The final appraisal and decision, however, lies with the purchaser.

BEFORE BUYING

An Oriental rug should be purchased as a work of art. Unfortunately, there are no absolutes that govern the purchase of an Oriental rug. There are, however, some basic guidelines that one should follow and questions that should be kept in mind.

What is the purpose of buying the Oriental rug? Is it utilitarian, for a decorative accent, a capital-gains investment, or a combination of several of these? If the purpose of the rug is strictly utilitarian, will the rug be in a heavy traffic pattern and how well can it be expected to withstand wear?

What is the area to be covered? Establish a minimum and maximum dimension suitable for the intended use of the rug. Rugs are usually paid for (whether quoted in this manner or not) on the basis of total number of square feet, or square meters. It is not economical to buy more rug than one needs.

What is the price range? The buyer should keep in mind the upper limit that he is willing to spend. Don't be pressured to buy a more expensive rug than the intended use warrants.

Is the price fair? Comparison shop! Rug prices can and do vary from dealer to dealer: rugs of the same type (Romanian rugs of the same Bucharest quality, for example), same age, and same size. Since sizes do vary, it is helpful to compute the cost per square foot or per square meter of each rug.

Can the rug be examined thoroughly? Often at auctions or house sales, hasty decisions are forced upon a prospective buyer before a careful inspection of a rug can be made. Objectionable flaws or damage, such as stains, moth damage, holes, slits in the foundation, or crooked edges may go unnoticed at a brief, first glance.

Can the rug be returned? A rug should be taken home on approval to see if it creates the desired effect. This is a standard practice among most reputable Oriental-rug dealers. Ask if the rug can be exchanged or returned for a full credit if the rug does not have the look desired when placed in your home.

Does the seller guarantee the rug? There are traveling auctions that may only be in town for several days. The buyer has no recourse if the rug purchased is misrepresented or has serious or objectionable flaws. At house sales, for example, the rug is sold "as is," and the seller assumes no responsibility.

Never be in such a hurry to buy an Oriental rug that you cannot carefully inspect the rug and evaluate its merits. A few extra minutes may save a lot of time, aggravation, and money, if it is later found that costly repairs need to be made.

BUYING

Bargaining

An Oriental rug may be purchased by making an offer lower than the stipulated or asking price, in much the same way as buying a house or a car. Bargaining is a compromise situation; in bargaining, knowledge is power. The final negotiated price can be strongly influenced by the knowledge of the buyer or seller.

Bargaining situations may be encountered almost anytime a person is trying to buy an Oriental rug, whether from an individual or a rug merchant. A rug dealer has certain costs that have been incurred and his prices tend to reflect current market conditions; therefore, his ability and willingness to bargain are somewhat restricted. An individual's price may have been set rather arbitrarily because of lack of market information and his minimal investment in the rug (the rug may have been inherited or held for some time).

Knowledge in any situation makes the position of the buyer more certain and strategically sound. The more knowledgeable the buyer, the more likely the compromise will be in his favor.

Buying at Auction

Many people are lured by the excitement of buying at auction. The hope of obtaining an Oriental rug for a fraction of its worth brings thousands of prospective buyers to auctions each year. The knowledgeable buyer may be able to make some good acquisitions, making careful selections from the wide range of rugs offered.

Buying an Oriental rug at *any* auction entails risks; the type and degree of risk varies with the kind of auction and with the knowledge of the buyer. The successful buyer not only has knowledge of rugs but also is familiar with the procedures and requirements of the auction. No rug purchased at an auction is returnable; the buyer rarely has any recourse if the rug is not as represented, is in need of repair, or if the buyer decides that he does not like it. It is difficult to properly inspect the condition of a rug, and rugs are sold on an "as is" basis.

There are three types of auctions: traveling or itinerant auctions, estate auctions, and those held at established auction houses. Each has its own attributes and benefits, as well as disadvantages.

TRAVELING AUCTIONS

Traveling auctions go from city to city, selling Oriental rugs in motels or other rented facilities. The auctioneers are master showmen and may have shills (their hired people in the audience) to bid the price up until an acceptable level has been reached. The rug will not be sold for less than a predetermined price that recovers all costs and yields a profit. Such costs include rent of the facility, auctioneer's commission, transportation costs, plus his cost of each rug.

A common misconception of the auction is that all rugs must be sold regardless of price. In the traveling auction, the auctioneer is under no such pressure; if bids do not exceed the auctioneer's minimum, that rug is withdrawn from consideration, to be offered again in the next city on the circuit.

Because of all these considerations, the risk is placed on the potential buyer, not on the auctioneer. Only on rare occasions is one able to purchase a rug for an amount less than its worth.

Many of the rugs sold at traveling auctions are rugs that for one reason or another don't sell on the wholesale market, or are wholesaler's rejects. Importers buy in lots, rather than buying individual rugs, so occasionally pieces are encountered that do not meet the wholesale standard of quality. Many of these rugs find their way to the auction block. Not all rugs at auctions are "inferior"; a few good rugs are often deliberately interspersed among the others.

ESTATE AUCTIONS

In an estate auction the entire furnishings of a specific household are liquidated. Unlike the traveling auctioneer, the estate auctioneer has been commissioned to dispose completely of all items, getting the most revenue possible. As a result, the potential buyer has a good chance of obtaining a rug for less than its value.

Yet risks are also present. At some estate sales, Oriental rugs are brought in to entice greater attendance. These rugs usually come from the stock of Oriental rug or antique dealers and are being sold at a preestablished minimum. In the traveling auction, the bidding is against the house; in the estate auction, one bids against other potential buyers, driving the price up. Rug dealers and other knowledgeable people are more apt to attend estate auctions, so competition can be fierce.

AUCTION HOUSES

Established auction houses have their reputations to maintain, as well as higher levels of costs to recoup. The potential buyer here bids against other bidders, but also against the house. The present owner of the rug to be sold has established the opening level for bids. Greater publicity usually attends the auctions of these houses, and collectors as well as dealers may come from afar.

Specialized collections and superior pieces are more likely to be offered by established auction houses because of their expertise, reputation, and ability to obtain the best possible prices for the owners. The prices obtained at these auctions will tend to reflect the actual worth of the rugs, and bargains should not be expected.

Knowledge is a prerequisite at any auction—ability to evaluate rug condition and knowledge of current prices and auction procedures are a must. Not only must the buyer be able to establish a realistic appraisal of what the rug may be worth on the market, he must also be able to set and observe a limit of what the rug is worth to him.

Purchasing Overseas

Knowledge and understanding of the area's or country's rugs is a necessity when one purchases an Oriental rug abroad. When away from home, buyers are at the mercy of the rug seller. There is little or no recourse if the rug is misrepresented.

Far too often, tourists who think they are getting "the buy of a lifetime" could have purchased the same rug at home for much less. The "silk" rug they purchased turns out to be a wool rug that has been given a luster wash, or the "antique" rug has been given a wash to make it appear old. In many cases the rug you purchased may not be the rug that is shipped to your home; a rug of much lesser quality may be substituted.

If you want to purchase an Oriental rug overseas, the best way is to do some comparison shopping at home before you leave. Check the prices of rugs from the countries that you will visit. You will have something with which to compare while abroad. Remember that there are a wide range of qualities and prices available from every country.

PLATE 10.1: *The back of a hand-knotted Indian carpet, woven in Jaipur.*

PLATE 10.2: *The back of a machine-made Oriental-design carpet.*

Keep in mind that the prices at your local Oriental rug retailer already include the freight charges, customs duty, and any applicable taxes. You will be liable for all of these in addition to your purchase price. In some instances, taxes and freight charges may amount to as much as, or even more than, the purchase price of the rug.

Trade agreements and duty charges vary from country to country, and are subject to change. Check with the proper governmental authorities about the duty or taxes imposed on Oriental rugs. Also verify the required documentation on rugs purchased as antique, and whether there are restrictions on rugs (antique) leaving a country.

Bargains can be found if you are willing to persevere and look for them. Before purchasing, check the prices in several shops; prices can vary greatly within the same bazaar. Bargaining should be done. Don't be pressured into paying more. If possible, take your purchase with you. Rugs can be baled into unbelievably small packages. Your rug might have a few wrinkles when you first get home, but these will eventually come out.

Some countries have government-operated handicraft stores. The prices here may be slightly higher than in a local bazaar, but you can generally be assured that the merchandise is as it is represented.

In China, Romania, and the Soviet Union, rugs may be purchased in stores operated for foreign visitors. The prices are fixed and there is no bargaining, but the merchandise is reasonably priced. Purchases in these stores usually cannot be made in local currency. Although some foreign currency may be disallowed, United States dollars, German deutschmarks, and Swiss francs usually are well received.

ORIENTAL-DESIGN RUGS

Rugs of Oriental design are widely available under numerous brand names. They have designs that have been copied from Persian, Chinese, and Turkoman carpets.

Oriental-design rugs are machine-made and must not be confused with genuine Oriental rugs. An Oriental rug *must* be hand made, either hand-knotted or hand-woven. An Oriental-*design* rug, since it is not an Oriental rug, will not maintain its value. Yet Oriental-design rugs often cost as much as, and sometimes more than, a genuine Oriental rug.

Four elements of carpet construction serve as checkpoints in determining whether a rug is a genuine Oriental or a machine-made imitation. These are the back, knots, fringed ends, and sides.

On the back of the machine-made carpet, the design is vague or indistinct; the hand-knotted rug has a design that is as well defined on the back as on the front (see Plates 10.1 and 10.2). At times inspecting the back

PLATE 10.3: *The pile of a Chinese rug has been split to show that each strand of wool has been tied to a pair of warp threads.*

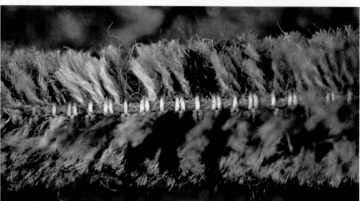

PLATE 10.4: *The pile of a machine-made carpet has been spread to show that the pile is attached without knots.*

PLATE 10.5: *The fringed end of a Romanian rug, Bucharesti quality.*

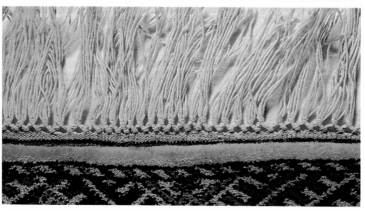

PLATE 10.6: *The fringed end of an Indian rug, woven in Jaipur.*

of the carpet is difficult because of a backing such as jute. This is a sure sign that the rug is *not* a genuine Oriental rug.

Fold the carpet and spread the pile; loops of yarn can be seen surrounding the warp threads in a genuine Oriental rug. The pile of a machine-made rug has been attached by either being stitched or glued (see Plates 10.3 and 10.4).

The fringe and selvedge offer other points for comparison. The fringe of a genuine Oriental rug is an extension of the carpet's warp threads; the manner in which the fringes are finished vary from one weaving center to another. The fringe of the machine-made rug has been overcast or sewn onto the carpet, and is not a part of the carpet's foundation. See Plates 10.5, 10.6, 10.7, and 10.8.

The sides, or selvedges, of the machine-made rugs are bound by machine, or serged, unlike the selvedges on the genuine Oriental rug (see Plates 10.9 and 10.10), which are hand-overcast in either cotton or wool.

It is necessary that all four elements of construction be checked before a final evaluation is made. Used Oriental rugs are occasionally found with sides that have been machine-serged or their ends refringed.

EVALUATING CONDITION AND DETERMINING VALUE

The carpet as a whole must be considered before making a detailed investigation of its component parts. If the colors are pleasing and the pattern well executed, then the potential buyer should check the carpet's structure.

Examining the Overall Carpet

Does the carpet lie flat on the floor? Wrinkles or ridges in the rug are caused by improper warp tension and will not come out; they wear rapidly as well as appearing unsightly. Creases caused by the rug's being folded and a slight rippling of the selvedge, however, will come out over a period of time.

Are the sides crooked, or are they relatively straight and parallel to each other? Some slight irregularities in the rug's sides are to be expected, but very crooked rugs are objectionable. Minor irregularities can be corrected by having the rug sized or stretched. This process should be done by the rug dealer before the rug is purchased. The rug should be carefully inspected afterward to ensure that the irregularities have been satisfactorily removed.

Each rug should be carefully inspected to make certain that no borders or portions of borders have been removed, especially the borders at the fringed ends of the rug. The rug should have the same border designs on all four sides and should not have been cut or shortened in any way. Turkoman and Turkoman-design rugs from India and Pakistan are the only exception, since they characteristically have dissimilar side and borders. See Chapter 7, p. 101.

The types of dyes and colors of the rug should be given careful consideration because of their effect on fading and running. Have the colors faded or will they run together when the rug is washed? Wiping a damp cloth over the top of a rug is a good test to determine if the dyes are colorfast. A rug in which the dyes have already run should be obvious by the blurred design. By comparing the colors on the front and back of the rug, one can tell whether or not the rug has faded. The back of a faded rug will be much darker than the sunlight-faded front. Aniline dyes will have produced all of these undesirable features, and rugs that have been colored with them should be avoided. See Chapter 2, p. 25 for a discussion of aniline dyes.

Age

Rugs may be classified into three age groups: new, semi-antique, and antique. A new rug is one that has never been used, although it can be several years old.

For practical purposes, many dealers classify rugs as semi-antique if they are from twenty-five to fifty years old, and as antique if they are more than fifty years old. Technically, a rug must be more than a hundred years old to be classified as an antique. Rugs that fall between the new and semi-antique classifications are termed "used." Their actual age and amount of use may vary considerably. The value of a used rug is generally less than its new and semi-antique counterparts, although it reacquires value with age.

Age does affect the value of a rug, but age must be considered together with condition. An antique rug that has been completely worn out is not valuable just because it is old. However, an antique rug in good condition can be priceless.

Structure

Examining the structure of any rug is important, yet for a *used* rug it is essential. A used rug will have had many opportunities to have been mis-

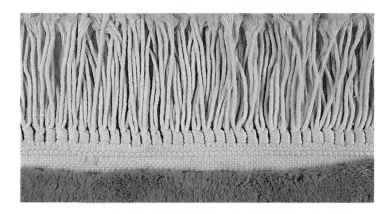

PLATE 10.7: *The fringed end of a Chinese rug.*

PLATE 10.8: *The overcast fringe of a machine-made Oriental-design rug. Fringes of this type will never be seen on a hand-knotted rug.*

PLATE 10.9: *The hand-overcast selvedge on a hand-knotted Indian rug, woven in Jaipur.*

PLATE 10.10: *The machine-stitched binding on the side of a machine-made Oriental-design rug. Note the running stitch that secures the selvedge to the body of the carpet.*

treated or improperly cared for. Many of the results of improper treatment are not immediately apparent on casual inspection.

In examining the structure of a rug, there are five major points to be checked. They are:

pile
warp and weft threads
fringe
selvedges
knots

PILE

The pile should be checked for worn areas, holes, and moth damage. Moth damage may appear on the top of the rug, the pile having been eaten down to the foundation; or it may be hidden on the back of the rug. The portion of the knot that is looped around the warp thread may also have been eaten. When this occurs, there is nothing securing the pile to the foundation of the rug. If this is suspected, one may easily remove a tuft of pile by pulling.

If the pile is well worn, the knots themselves are visible. This may occur in spots, rather than uniformly over all the surface of the rug, as when caused by heavy traffic patterns.

In the pile of older rugs, white knots are sometimes visible. These are knots in the warp or weft threads. All rugs have them, but they are more noticeable in older rugs with low pile. If these are objectionable, they can easily be touched up with any colorfast dye.

Chinese and Chinese-design rugs woven in India often have pile that has been carved or sculptured around the designs and motifs. This should not be confused with moth damage.

If dead or skin wool (see Chapter 2, p. 21) has been used for the pile, the fibers will be brittle and not wear well. In a used rug, worn spots caused by the dead wool will be quite obvious. In a new rug, dead wool can be felt by running one's hand across the pile; the dead wool has a definite coarse, bristly feel. Rugs are rarely woven entirely of dead wool.

WARP AND WEFT THREADS

The warp and the weft threads should be checked for cuts and breaks. The rug should be turned completely over to facilitate this inspection. The cuts or breaks in the warp and weft threads can become serious if not repaired *before* the rug is purchased.

FRINGE

An inspection of the fringe should be made to determine if the fringe is the original, or if a replacement fringe has been added. Folding a rug back at the end of the pile is the best way to check whether the fringe is an un-broken extension of the warp threads. In a refringed rug the warp threads will terminate (either by being cut or turned under) and a fringed band attached. A refringed rug is less valuable than a rug with its original fringe, even if the original fringe is not in particularly good condition.

SELVEDGES

The selvedges bind the sides (terminal warp threads) of the carpet. They do not wear as quickly as the fringe but do on occasion need to be reovercast. The reovercasting should always be done by hand rather than machine.

KNOTS

The *jufti*, or false knot, has been used in some Indian rugs. The knot is tied around four warp threads instead of the usual two. See Chapter 2, p. 22, *jufti* knot.

KNOT COUNT

A feature basic to the construction of all Oriental rugs is the tightness of weave, usually referred to as a rug's "knot count." This is simply the number of knots in a given area, and is quoted either in knots per square inch or per square meter. The number of knots per square inch may vary from as few as 10 to as many as 500, while knots per square meter may range from 16,000 to 800,000. Figure 10-A converts knots per square inch to knots per square meter and vice versa. Knot count can be an important tool in evaluating the quality of an Oriental rug—but only when it is properly used.

The assumption quite often made is that "the higher the knot count, the better or more desirable the rug." This is generally true, but there are too many factors involved for this statement always to be accurate.

An antique Khotan rug from the Xinjiang province of China will be more valuable than an Indian carpet of the same knot count, age, and condition, simply because Khotan rugs are more scarce. Knot count should be used only when comparing rugs from the same weaving center, in the same condition, and of the same age. Each rug possesses its own attributes and is unique unto itself, further complicating comparisons between rugs.

Several countries have a different way of denoting the quality of their Oriental rugs. In China, the term *line* (e.g., 90 line) is used. In Pakistan, the knot count is given in the form of a formula (e.g., 11/22). Each of these methods can be converted to the more common number of knots per square inch.

The number associated with the term *line* is the number of pairs of warp threads per linear foot; this in turn is the same as the number of knots per linear foot. A 90-line rug has 90 knots per linear foot, both horizontally and vertically, which is equivalent to approximately 54 knots per square inch (90/12 x 90/12 = 54). The knot count of a Pakistani rug can be figured by multiplying the numbers of the formula by each other (11/22 becomes 11 × 22, or 242 knots per square inch). The first number indicates how many horizontal knots there are in a linear inch; the second number indicates the number of vertical knots in a linear inch.

Each weaving center has its own characteristic range of knot counts (see Appendix). Individual rugs from the same weaving center, however, do vary in knot count. Romanian rugs are given labels or "brand" names that are assigned according to the quality of the rug (see Figure 8-B).

Knot count is calculated by counting the number of loops (knot backs) that fall within a 1-inch (or 1-meter) square. Lay a ruler along a weft thread on the back of the rug; count the number of knots in an inch (meter).

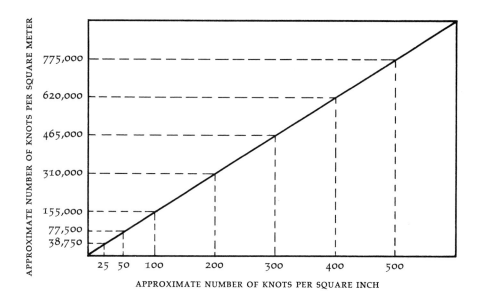

FIGURE 10-A: *KNOT-COUNT CONVERSION CHART*

To convert knots per square inch to knots per square meter, find the approximate number of knots per square inch along the horizontal axis of Figure 10-A. Draw an imaginary line (or follow one of the lines provided) to the heavy diagonal line, then draw an imaginary line from that point of intersection to the vertical axis and read the approximate number of knots per square meter. To convert knots per square meter to knots per square inch, reverse the procedure. For example, a rug with 200 knots per square inch has approximately 310,000 knots per square meter.

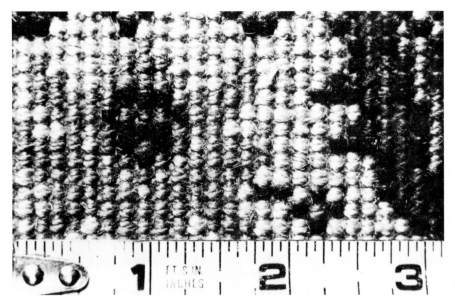

PLATE 10.11: *Counting knots per square inch on the back of a carpet.*

(When knots are tied on warp threads on the same level, each knot will have two loops clearly visible.) Multiplying the two numbers together gives the number of knots per square inch (meter). This should be done in five different areas scattered over the back of the rug, and those results averaged.

Rugs with higher knot counts have a denser pile than those with lower knot counts. A dense pile gives a sturdier, more durable rug. The pile of high-knot-count rugs is usually cut shorter, yielding a crisp design. These rugs are relatively more expensive than those with lower knot counts.

Each of the points discussed does affect the value of a rug, and the price should reflect the overall condition of the rug. A small flaw that might be objectionable to one person is not always objectionable to another. Since Oriental rugs are individually handcrafted, minor flaws will usually be found; absolute perfection should not be expected. If a rug has a deficiency, it is important that the purchaser be aware of the flaw and how it affects the rug's value; such information is necessary for an informed decision.

CARE

Oriental rugs require surprisingly little care. Dirt does not penetrate these rugs, as it does machine-made carpeting, although soil will eventually work its way to the base of the pile. Depending on the amount of traffic they undergo, rugs should be cleaned every three to five years. Cleaning should be done by a reputable firm that specializes in the cleaning of Oriental rugs. Proper cleaning is essential; steam-cleaning, dry-cleaning, and certain chemical processes remove the natural oils and cause the pile to become brittle and wear more rapidly.

In the regular vacuuming of Oriental rugs, the vacuum cleaner should move in the same direction as the nap of the carpet. The direction of the nap can be determined by running the hand across the pile (from fringe to fringe). Vacuuming against the grain presses the dirt back into the carpet. The fringe of a carpet should never be vacuumed, but swept with a broom. The continued catching of the fringe in the suction of a vacuum causes it to break and tear. Sweeping the carpet with a broom also helps bring out the natural patina or sheen in the rug.

Oriental rugs have the remarkable ability to withstand wear. Their life span is at least three or four times that of machine-made commercial carpeting. A good-quality pad helps protect the rug and prolongs its life even more. The best padding for an Oriental rug is hair- or fiber-filled with rubberized surfaces to keep the rug from moving or wrinkling.

Spills of virtually any nature may be removed without permanent stain if taken care of in time. Dilute the spill with plenty of water, and blot the wet area until *all* of the moisture is removed. Failure to remove all of the moisture might result in mildew.

Moths can cause extensive damage to Oriental rugs. Not only do moths eat the pile but they also eat the knots on the back of the rug. Moths are especially attracted to dark, relatively undisturbed areas, such as those under furniture. It is quite simple to eliminate these pests and safeguard against their return. Both the front and back of a carpet should be sprayed about every six months with any one of a number of moth sprays available on the market.

If a rug or carpet needs to be stored, it should be mothproofed, rolled (not folded), and put in a dry, moth-free environment.

The leakage of potted plants can inflict costly damage on an Oriental rug. The constant seepage or condensation of water on the bottom of the pot causes the foundation and the pile to rot. Never place a potted plant on an Oriental rug and be very cautious about placing a plant near one.

Repairs

Repairs may be necessary during the life of an Oriental rug, but they should be undertaken only by an expert. Common minor repairs include having the fringed ends secured and reinforced, or the selvedges reovercast; these are relatively inexpensive and should be done in order to prevent the loss, knot by knot, of the pile. Even minor repairs, such as worn fringe or selvedge, can rapidly develop into a serious problem.

Repairing holes in the warp and weft threads, or reweaving moth-damaged areas of the pile, can be done but may be quite costly. This should be done only after consideration of how much the rug is worth. An excellent repair should not be detected with a casual glance. If in doubt about the qualifications of a repairer, ask to see examples of his finished repair work.

As with any work or work of art, an Oriental rug must have proper care.

Oriental rugs are not only beautiful, they are also the most practical home furnishing you can buy. They enhance any decor with their beauty, and make a room an individual creation. Given proper care, the Oriental rug will be a durable floor covering as well as a treasured work of art.

APPENDIX

Summary Chart of Oriental Rugs, by Availability, Durability, Price, Typical Knot Count, and Common Rug Sizes

LEGEND: In the columns headed "Availability," "Durability," and "Price," the numbers express the relative availability, durability, and price of the rugs listed; a *1* indicates a rug that is *not* relatively available or durable, and is of *low* price. A *5* indicates a rug that is relatively widely available, is very durable, and of high price. Availability is further divided into AM. for the American market and EUR. for the European market.

| | | AVAILABILITY | | DURABILITY | PRICE | TYPICAL KNOT COUNT (KNOTS PER SQUARE INCH) | | | | | COMMON RUG SIZES | | |
		AM.	EUR.			LESS THAN 50	51–150	151–250	251–350	MORE THAN 350	2 X 4 FT. OR SMALLER	3 X 5 TO 6 X 9 FT.	8 X 10 FT. OR LARGER
CHINA													
	70 line	3	4	3	3	x					x	x	x
	90 line	5	5	4	4		x				x	x	x
	120 line	2	4	5	4			x			x	x	x
	240 line	1	3	5	5				x		x	x	x
	Xinjiang	1	3	3	3	x					x	x	
TIBET													
	"Lhasas"	1	1	3	2	x						x	
NEPAL													
	"Tibetan"	1	1	4	1	x						x	

152

		AVAILABILITY		DURABILITY	PRICE	TYPICAL KNOT COUNT (KNOTS PER SQUARE INCH)					COMMON RUG SIZES		
		AM.	EUR.			LESS THAN 50	51–150	151–250	251–350	MORE THAN 350	2 X 4 FT. OR SMALLER	3 X 5 TO 6 X 9 FT.	8 X 10 FT. OR LARGER
INDIA													
	Agra	1	2	3	3		x	x			x	x	
	Jaipur	3	4	4	3			x			x	x	x
	Mirzapur/ Bhadohi												
	Srinagar (Kashmir)	2	3	4	4			x	x		x	x	
PAKISTAN													
	Persian Weave	3	3	4	4			x	x	x		x	
	Mori Weave												
	single-ply	4	4	4	3		x	x	x		x	x	x
	double-ply	3	3	3	3		x				x	x	x
ROMANIA													
	Brăila	3	4	3	2		x				x	x	x
	Bran	1	2	2	2		x					x	x
	Brașov	1	2	3	3		x					x	x
	Bucharesti	5	5	3	2		x				x	x	x
	Dorna	1	1	1	1	x						x	x
	Harmon	3	4	3	3		x					x	x
	Milcov	1	2	5	4				x				x
	Mureș	3	4	4	4			x				x	x
	Olt	1	3	4	4			x				x	x
	Postavarul	1	1	3	3			x					x
	Transylvania	2	3	2	3		x					x	

* Variations in durability and price are extreme, depending on quality. Index numbers should be regarded as an average only.

GLOSSARY OF TERMS

ABRASH   a color variation or stripe of a slightly different hue across the body of the carpet. This is the result of a slight color difference in the dye lots used.

ARA-KHACHI   middle or main stripe in the border (*see* Bala-Khachi).

AUBUSSON   a pileless (flat-weave) rug that was once hand-woven in France, with pastel colors.

AY GUL   moon-shaped motif used as the medallion in rugs from eastern Turkestan.

BAFF   the Persian word for *knot*.

BALA-KHACHI   small border on either side of the main border (*see* Ara-Khachi).

BOTEH   a small motif that resembles a pine cone or pear (*see* Figure 3-A, p. 30).

BRAILA   quality of Romanian rug with a knot count of 160,000 knots per square meter (103 knots per square inch), woven with a cotton foundation.

BUCHARESTI   quality of Romanian rug with a knot count of 110,000 knots per square meter (70 knots per square inch), woven with a cotton foundation.

BUKHARA   name associated with Turkoman Gul-design rugs woven in India and Pakistan; also, an ancient marketplace for the rugs from Turkestan.

CARTOON   a piece of graphlike paper on which the rug pattern has been drawn. It is used as a guide in weaving a rug; each square represents a single knot, its color being keyed to the color of the square (*see* talim).

CARVED PILE   grooves cut into the pile to further accentuate the borders and designs. This is done in some Chinese and Indian carpets.

CAUCASIAN   refers to rugs woven in the Caucasus Mountain region of the Soviet Union. The patterns of these rugs are brightly colored, highly stylized, and geometrical.

CLOSED BACK   a term referring to the appearance of the back of a Chinese carpet. The weft threads of a closed back carpet are not visible when the carpet is observed from the back; the knots completely cover them.

DHURRIE   a pileless carpet, usually woven in India with either cotton or wool. The design is created by interweaving colored weft threads through the warp threads.

DORNA   quality of Romanian rug with a knot count of 40,000 knots per square meter (25 knots per square inch), woven with a cotton foundation.

DOZAR   refers to carpets of the 4 by 6 foot size.

DRUGGET   a pileless carpet; very coarsely woven, usually of cotton. They are made in India.

EMBOSSED   sculptured, or pile that has been woven longer than the rest of the ground and then trimmed to give a relief effect.

FRINGE   the loose ends of a carpet's warp threads, emerging from the upper and lower ends of the carpet; they may be either knotted or plain.

GABBA not considered a genuine Oriental rug. A woolen-fabric rug with designs that have been embroidered onto the wool. They are made in India.

GHIORDES KNOT *see* Turkish knot.

GUL Turkoman tribal emblem, once unique to the Turkoman tribe that wove them. Different Turkoman tribal *guls* have been adopted by the weaving centers of India and Pakistan.

HARMON quality of Romanian rug with a knot count of 200,000 knots per square meter (129 knots per square inch), woven with a woolen foundation.

HATCHLOU originally a Turkoman design, in which the field is divided into quadrants by wide bars or stripes.

HERATI pattern consisting of a small rosette, generally found inside a diamond shape, surrounded by four leaves or "fish."

JUFTI KNOT a modified Turkish or Persian knot, in which the weaver uses four warp threads per knot instead of two.

KELIM a pileless carpet created by interweaving colored weft threads through the warp threads; or, a finished terminal portion of a carpet falling between the pile and the fringe.

LINE a term referring to the number of pairs of warp threads, or knots per linear foot.

MIHRAB the arch or niche of a Prayer rug.

MORI refers to a type of weave used in India and Pakistan. The Persian knot is tied on a pair of warp threads that are on the same level.

MURES quality of Romanian carpet with a knot count of 200,000 knots per square meter (129 knots per square inch), woven with a cotton foundation.

NAMDA not considered to be a genuine Oriental rug. They are made in India of felt; the design is either appliquéd onto the felt or made by dyed wool being pressed into the rug during the felting process.

OLT quality of Romanian rug with a knot count of 250,000 knots per square meter (160 knots per square inch), woven with a cotton foundation.

OPEN BACK a term referring to the appearance of the back of a Chinese carpet. The weft threads of an open back carpet are clearly visible when observing the back of the carpet.

PANEL DESIGN design in which the field is divided into rectilinear compartments, each of which encloses one or more motifs.

PATINA the natural silken sheen that comes to a carpet with age.

PERSIAN KNOT sometimes called the Senna knot; a strand of wool encircles one warp thread and winds loosely around the other.

PILE nap of the rug; the clipped ends of the knotted wool.

POSTAVARUL the finest-quality Romanian carpet woven with a woolen foundation. The knot count is 240,000 knots per square meter (155 knots per square inch).

SAFF a multiple Prayer design, with two or more *mihrabs* arranged in a series.

SAVONNERIE a rug hand-knotted in France, with a thick, heavy pile and pastel colors. New copies are being woven in India.

SCOARTA a pileless carpet, or kelim, woven in Romania.

SCULPTURED PILE pile that has been embossed or woven longer than the rest of the ground and then trimmed to give a relief effect.

SELVEDGE the sides or edges of a carpet, usually overcast with wool for reinforcement.

SENNA KNOT *see* Persian knot.

SHAH ABBAS patron of Persian carpet-weaving (1571–1629); also an all-over design with various types of palmettes, cloud-bands, and vases interconnected by some form of vines or tendrils.

SHOU Chinese character that symbolizes long life.

SKIRT an additional panel or band woven at the top and bottom of most Turkoman-design rugs.

SPANDREL the portion of the Prayer rug that appears above and on either side of the *mihrab* (*see* Plate 3.10).

SWASTIKA Chinese symbol meaning luck.

TALIM a piece of paper on which the design of a carpet has been written out, in a type of script.

TRANSYLVANIA quality of Romanian carpet with a knot count of 121,000 knots per square meter (79 knots per square inch), woven on a woolen foundation.

TURKISH KNOT Ghiordes knot; a strand of wool that encircles two warp threads, with the loose ends drawn tightly between the two.

TURKOMAN refers to rugs from the Turkestan region; their patterns are made up of repeated *guls* (small geometric motifs), which were once unique to each Turkoman tribe.

WARP threads running longitudinally through the carpet; knots are tied to the warp threads.

WEFT threads running horizontally (perpendicular to the warp threads); these are used to secure the knots in place.

FOR FURTHER READING

GENERAL

Dilley, A. U. *Oriental Rugs and Carpets*, rev. ed. by M. S. Diamond (New York: Lippincott, 1959).

Erdmann, Kurt. *Oriental Carpets* (Basingstoke, England: The Crosby Press, 1976).

Ferrero, Mercedes Viale (trans.). *Rare Carpets from East and West* (London: Orbis Books, 1972).

Fokker, Nicolas. *Oriental Carpets for Today* (Garden City, N. Y.: Doubleday & Co., Inc., 1973).

Formenton, Fabio. *Oriental Rugs and Carpets* (New York: McGraw-Hill, 1972).

Franses, Jack. *European and Oriental Rugs* (New York: Arco Publishing Co., Inc., 1970).

Gans-Ruedin, E. *The Connoisseur's Guide to Oriental Carpets* (Rutland, Vt.: Tuttle, 1971).

Harris, Nathaniel. *Rugs and Carpets of the Orient* (London: Hamlyn, 1977).

Herbert, Janice S. *Oriental Rugs: The Illustrated Guide* (New York: Macmillan Publishing Co., Inc., 1978).

Hubel, Reinhard G. *The Book of Carpets* (New York: Praeger Publishers, 1970).

Jacobsen, Charles. *Oriental Rugs* (Rutland, Vt.: Tuttle, 1962).

Jacobsen, Charles. *Oriental Rugs: An Updated Guide* (Syracuse, N. Y.: Jacobsen, Inc., 1977).

Larson, Knut. *Rugs and Carpets of the Orient* (London: Frederick Warne and Co., Ltd., 1966).

Reed, Stanley. *All Color Book of Oriental Carpets and Rugs* (New York: Crescent Books, 1972).

Schlosser, Ignaz. *The Book of Rugs: Oriental and European* (New York: Bonanza Books, 1963).

CHINESE

Hackmack, Adolf. *Chinese Carpets and Rugs* (New York: Dover Publications, Inc., 1973).

Lorentz, H. A. *A View of Chinese Rugs* (London: Routledge and Kegan Paul, 1972).

Tiffany Studios. *Antique Chinese Rugs* (Rutland, Vt.: Tuttle, 1976).

TIBET

Denwood, Philip. *The Tibetan Carpet* (Warminster, England: Aris & Phillips Ltd., 1974).

EASTERN TURKESTAN

Bidder, Hans. *Carpets from Eastern Turkestan* (London: Zwemmer, 1964).

ROMANIA

Petrescu, P., and Rodna N. *Romanian Textiles* (Leigh-on-Sea, England: F. Lewis Ltd., 1966).

INDIA

Chattopadhyaya, K. *Carpets & Floor Coverings of India* (Bombay, India: Russi Jal Taraporevala, 1976).

INDEX
Boldface numbers refer to illustration pages